FASHION 85

THE MUST-HAVE BOOK FOR FASHION INSIDERS

FASHION 85

ISBN 0 312 28394 – 6

First U.S. Edition
10 9 8 7 6 5 4 3 2 1

Cover and Design by Neil Dell

FASHION 85

THE MUST-HAVE BOOK FOR FASHION INSIDERS

EDITED BY EMILY WHITE
UK COMMISSIONING EDITOR MAXIM JAKUBOWSKI
US COMMISSIONING EDITOR ANN CARLI

ST. MARTIN'S PRESS,
175 FIFTH AVENUE, NEW YORK, NY 10010

CONTENTS

THE
LONDON
COLLECTIONS
Sheridan McCoid

● **At last. As models paced the runways in London this spring showing a complete spectrum of talents for Autumn/Winter 84, so everyone acknowledged the fact that after a very long time in the doldrums, London fashion was again ready to stand up and be counted. An unheard of number of foreign press and buyers, particularly from America, made the trip from Milan before going on to Paris in order to pass judgement.**

Mrs Thatcher hosted a cocktail party at 10 Downing Street at the end of the week, an unprecedented admission that the British fashion industry represents trade for the country and therefore deserves some recognition and government support: both Paris and Milan have had government backing and approval for years. At the end of it all, Norman Tebbitt, Secretary of State for Trade and Industry, announced a new £20 million investment scheme to help small firms in the textiles, clothing, knitting and footwear industries to buy new machinery and keep up with advancing technology. And there was more good news to follow. The Design Advisory Service Funded Consultancy Scheme will be extended, providing subsidised consultancy on all aspects of product design to companies within the clothing industry; there are plans for Royal Society of Arts bursaries to place design graduates in industry and for a Register of Apparel Designers to be set up, funded by industry and government to give small companies access to design expertise. All this at the end of a well planned and organised week of shows and exhibitions, all situated within an easy square mile of each other.

The seeds for the success of this spring's collections were sown last autumn when the Spring-Summer 84 Collections were shown. British fashion has always had a rather eccentric reputation with foreign press and buyers. Plenty of ideas, imagination and flair – a marvellous breeding

● KATHARINE HAMNETT

● BODYMAP

ground of designs to be picked over, adapted and rushed back home – but nothing to be taken too seriously.

Outside this country the only aspect of British fashion worthy of copy, photos or simply plain interest was "Street Fashion". Newspapers and magazines in Paris, New York and Milan all had a great time documenting the crazy antics of young London as it paraded along the King's

Road. Here too, the story of the street kids was bled dry and indeed plenty of exciting things were and still are going on there. But that has changed.

Last October London pulled itself together and laid the cards on the table. Fashion PR Lynne Franks who has for a long time been fighting hard for the British fashion industry, organised the Murjani sponsorship and a handful of designers showed

NIALL McINERNY

their collections under tarpaulin in a marquee set up in the grounds of the Commonwealth Institute – a solid step forward in bringing us into line with our international competitors on the presentation level – the Paris collections are shown in a series of vast tents erected in the gardens of the Louvre.

Darlings of that particular week were the BodyMap pair Stevie Stewart and David Holah who showed only briefly with the Individual Clothes Show but managed to cause quite a stir with their "*Querelle* meets Olive Oyl" collection of loose, unexpected shapes, soft textures and bold anchor prints.

For the first time Wendy Dagworthy put her collection on the runway – easy, asymmetric, hip-swathed clothes in beige, white and black panels of soft wool or linen weaved simply in and out of the spot lights.

Sheridan Barnett's growing reputation for long and square cuts of linen, cotton and wool in solid blocks of colour was reiterated in simple dresses, ankle skimming skirts with square tops and broad shouldered trench coats. The Individual Clothes Show, as usual a mixed bag, provided a necessary platform for up and coming talent, an airing for some "already there" talent and an unfortunate waste of space for those clothes best left on the dress rail.

Helen Robinson received a well deserved, even belated pat on the

● SHERIDAN BARNETT

● BETTY JACKSON

● JASPER CONRAN

head for a collection of swinging, clinging cotton ribs and jerseys in black, grey, cream and – fluorescent – the hot pink, green or orange splash of colour popular for summer and a welcome injection to a perpetually monochrome palette. Helen owns and designs for PX, the shop in Covent Garden that was put on the map a few years ago: she produced the first of the frilly white shirts at the start of the Romantic/pirate phase when the likes of Adam Ant dressed up in all their swashbuckling gear. Alongside Katharine Hamnett, Helen must be one of the designers who has suffered most from the crude ripping-off and imitating that goes on in the fashion business – so, timely recognition for young British talent.

In general, the feeling last October for what we'd all be wearing in the summer was for loose and relaxed clothes, more often very long with plenty of hip emphasis – drop waists, jacket lengths, belts. Fabrics were linen and cotton in plain or stripes with a few bold African prints in deeper colours although black, white, cream, navy and grey dominated the colour chart with splashes of scarlet, shocking pink and orange.

So those were the designer predictions and the press interpretations of the designs. It is always interesting to sit back during the months after the collections and watch the way that certain looks are picked up by the industry and, just as unpredictably, certain looks are instantly discarded.

Inspired by social changes, topical events, whims and trends that the fanciful fashion business is always the first to absorb, it is impossible to predict further than shapes and colours. For example, on the runways there were plenty of long, loose cotton or linen shifts often with a drop waist and box pleating in cream, white and pastel shades. This spring saw a rush of media attention focused on India – the long running television series *The Jewel in the Crown*, *The Far Pavilions* and the making of the film *A Passage to India* all encouraged romantic notions of those last days of the Raj. And so the two were blended. Those simple linen frocks were given the India treatment, either photographed there, in India, or accessorised with the right shoes and hats, bringing a glimpse of stylish British women staying fresh and cool in the steamy heat of it all in magazine pages and shop windows.

Sportswear had passed through a transitionary phase the previous summer and all the paraphernalia of a sporting life is nowadays seen sitting around in pubs and restaurants as often as it is in changing rooms. This summer though, the look has been much harsher than last year's pastels – black and fluorescent with bold lettering. A boost by Olympic fever kept the look truly sporty and a spring heatwave brought bright singlets and shorts out onto the streets – along with the five rings of the Olympic logo, which was set to stay all summer,

- SHERIDAN BARNETT
- LAURENCE
- KATHARINE HAMNETT
- CHRISSIE WALSH

NIALL MCINERNY

NIALL MCINERNY

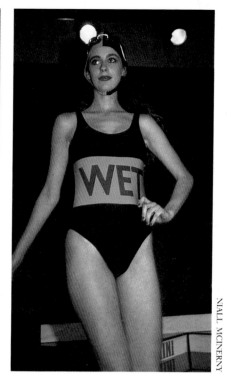

of course.

Trendy Londoners picked up on cycling gear at the beginning of the summer and, with no cycles in sight, brightly coloured Raleigh tops were worn with jaunty peaked caps and Lonsdale sports boots.

From Norma Kamali's cotton jersey tights, overprinted white on black washing instructions to "WET" swimwear, "VIVE" sweatshirting and Bo Bo Kaminsky "MADE SOME-WHERE IN ITALY" cropped tops, lettering took off this summer. Nothing like the discreet designer logos of previous years, but loud and eye-catching.

The places to go to find out what fashionable Londoners are buying are the shops they frequent. During the early summer, Jones in the King's Road who stock BodyMap, PX, No? Yes! and shoes by Palladium and Freelance among others, had rails of BodyMap cotton fluted skirts selling out as soon as they were re-ordered, the same too for tubular ribbed skirts by PX – all in white and cream. And Whistles, who have five branches around central London, were doing their best to keep up with a demand for sweatshirting and cotton jersey and in particular Bo Bo Kaminsky white sweats, Laurence pants and tops and Naf Naf crumpled cotton cardi-gans and pants. Colours here too were predominantly white and cream and the only accessory was the wide leather or rubber belt to be slung around layers of unironed linen. All very relaxed, just as the designers had predicted over six months previously.

With the bones of a better organised London Fashion Week to play with, it wasn't then surprising that the Autumn collections held in March were so successful, though admittedly the whole package could have swung either way. But thanks to determination and enthusiasm from all quarters, everything worked beautifully.

London finally shook off its provincial image. The Murjani Designer Focus tent was sited once again in the grounds of the Commonwealth Institute and many more designers showed their collections there. And whereas before the exhibition stands were displayed in various stuffy hotel suites, and Olympia was a seedy jungle of stands and walkways to be waded through, everything but Mainseason was held at Olympia which had been given a total face lift. The London Designer Collections were spaciously displayed but a few paces from Design Studio, Individual Clothes Show and other rails worthy of note.

Even the Princess of Wales took a trip around the stands of her favoured designers. Her particular clique are not to be ignored for she still holds tremendous influence over a corner of the industry that she single-handedly revived. Classics for younger women were not considered fashionable until the Princess started to wear them in her own way. It is difficult though to dress at such a stylish pace for very long, especially when the eyes of the

● BODYMAP

● BODYMAP

● BETTY JACKSON

world are always on you and last winter found the Princess dressing in a more typically royal and safe way than we had seen previously. Jasper Conran, a favourite of the Princess, showed pretty and stylish collections for both autumn and winter. Dresses were popular in bright, loose silks and ruched cottons, along with the traditional wrap coat dress in cream linen or fine navy wool. The Autumn collection was very classic. Cropped jackets, tiny waists and long slim skirts looked stunning as did the purple leather separates at the beginning of the show.

Arabella Pollen who showed her first collection only a few seasons ago, has done amazingly well and last winter the Princess wore fitted tweed and velvet suits and coats designed by her.

The Princess invariably chooses her wardrobe from London-based designers and her patronage has certainly helped to put British fashion back on the map. Another area of design we have to thank the Princess for helping to improve, is maternity wear which has lost some of its "huge floral smock" image since the Princess managed to look charming and stylish throughout her first pregnancy and this summer saw Jasper Conran's first collection for Mothercare go into the shops.

The shows themselves this spring were full of vitality and coming from the quieter, slightly conservative runways of Milan, everyone seemed pleased that there was so much to say and see and photograph. Colour was used with abandon to make vivid statements on the runways.

Katharine Hamnett kicked off the week with her show. The "Acid Rain Rap" was followed by a zippy collection of crumpled cotton and bruised silk in familiar white, khaki, grey, navy and black. "Save the World" tee shirts jostled with "Worldwide Nuclear Ban Now" sweats as Katharine did her bit – all profits from the sales of the slogan tee shirts will go to a charity that Katharine is hoping to set up herself to fight child abuse. A welcome rainbow of bright, bright blues, reds and emeralds rounded off the show with padded parkas, fine silk tops and skirts and fluttery lengths of colour to wrap, tie and drape.

Betty Jackson, showing for the first time on her own, went for the wide shouldered, long and lean look that swanked confidently along the runways in shades of bitter chocolate with yellow and stripey jersey under huge felt bowlers and over tight woollen leggings. Apart from wool she used leather for the first time – soft, voluminous coats and jackets. Always popular with Betty and those who buy her clothes were the long jackets and cardigans which looked as strong as ever worn over tubular skirts and V-front sweater dresses for next winter.

Owing to their success last season, BodyMap drew the largest crowd to the Murjani tent for a show which was, shall we say, different. Helen

● HELEN ROBINSON FOR PX

● WORLDS END

● BETTY JACKSON

● WENDY DAGWORTHY

NIALL MCINERNY

NIALL MCINERNY

14

Terry from Culture Club launched it all with her wondrously powerful voice resonating around the tent. And from there, nothing stopped. Both designers' mothers had been roped in, as had assorted children and friends who all tottered along the runway with the models in high wedge canvas lace boots. The collection, entitled "The Cat in the Hat takes a Rumble with the Techno Fish", had a fishy theme running all the way through. There were white gloves with long tentacle fingers, black and white tube dresses with portholes cut into the sides and jazzy starfish prints. Cotton jersey boxer shorts were worn over bold hooped tights with cropped wrap knit tops and double hats and short skating skirts with hoods all bobbed along together in a mess of red, white and black.

Sheridan Barnett's show started with a swirl of colour as a model dressed in a huge red cloak flounced along the runway. Sheridan invariably borrows keenly from the man's wardrobe and this collection was no exception with crisp square and tailored flannel suits in dark colours worn over classic shirts. There were plenty of coats – fur lined, velvet edged and tweeds, both fitted and loose. Working mostly in earthy tones of browns and mushroom with the odd splash of violet and red, Sheridan's was a collection of long lines and uncluttered shapes.

The Individual Clothes Show, though long, had pockets of very interesting clothes, some of which are worth a mention. Rumour had it that Laurence was a stylish young designer from Paris. In fact he is a stylish lad from Liverpool who saw what was in the shops, decided that he didn't like it and so went into business himself. His layered white sweatshirting looked fresh for winter on the runway. In contrast, Traffic News, a Japanese company, showed solid black. Although we seem to have seen more than enough black over the past few seasons, the Japanese have a way of cutting and layering that makes it look different and still new. Susan Backhouse, a relative newcomer, showed a collection of stripey sportswear and No? Yes! presented a *Day at the Races* feel with cropped wool jackets and trousers.

Wendy Dagworthy, whose clothes are often bright and easy, showed a particularly vibrant collection this time. Mohair wool coats, wide cropped jackets, back buttoning smocks and circular skirts were all muddled in together in a blaze of fuchsia, scarlet and orange. For men, the mohair jackets were spared none of the colour, same too for the suits.

So, if all the promises of more money and support are fulfilled then the struggle to sit on top alongside our European competitors is almost over. A few more solid Fashion Weeks to let everyone know that London means business and from then on it will all be plain sailing. Well, something like that.

● BODYMAP

THE PARIS COLLECTIONS

Jackie Moore

● The French have long considered themselves to be the leaders in the world of fashion. There is no historical basis for this belief but then the truth has seldom been allowed to hold back a cause. In the past, fashion sprang from the courts, with Italy, France and England jostling for the number one position and Spain throwing in a new fashion idea, like the farthingale, as an occasional diversion. Gradually Paris assumed, as if by right, the central role and has clung onto it ever since.

Today, the designers of London, New York, Milan and Tokyo may each lay claim to be arbiters of world taste but the French answer with one of those Gallic shrugs of the shoulder. And there is no doubt that it is still Paris that attracts the largest crowds.

Mind you, there is a certain sneakiness in the French approach. By maintaining the Paris myth they have managed to attract the cream of international design, who journey to Paris to show their new collections, make their name and sustain the image of France as the centre of the fashion world.

The major protagonists of the 1984 shows have included the German Karl Lagerfeld, the Italian Valentino and a whole clutch of Japanese, led by Issey Miyake, but the end result is that international attention is focussed on Paris, whatever her own designers are producing.

If there are also strong collections coming out of the French houses then that is a bonus and there is no question that the home team faced up to the competition pretty well during the year.

The greatest asset of the French, and one that shines through the collections, is confidence. They lost it, once, during the 1960s, during the all too brief flowering of British ready-to-wear, but in no time at all they found their strength again. It lies in a belief in themselves, not quite arrogance, and it is based on the experience and solid background of the couture.

The established names of the

CHRIS MOORE

French couture have been around for many years. Even the young master himself, Yves St Laurent, is celebrating 25 years with his own house. The couture group know all about survival and presentation, and they are accustomed to the limelight. Each season Yves St Laurent, Dior, Givenchy, Ungaro et al produce professionally put together collections that sell all over the world even when they do not fill the fashion papers.

Some of the best of the ready-to-wear designers have worked in the couture studios, like Karl Lagerfeld at Jean Patou or Issey Miyake at Givenchy. The confidence born of experience has rubbed off on them.

Above all, they understand all about attracting attention. Nando Miglio's show productions in Milan have all the chic. Zandra Rhodes and Antony Price do their best to stun their audiences but when it comes to spectacle and sheer drama there is nothing to touch the Paris collections.

It is this as much as anything that has stemmed the tide of the Japanese takeover that threatened to overwhelm everyone by the end of last year. The eternal drumming and monotony of the Japanese presentations, the aggressive stance of the models, the lack of warmth has had a stultifying effect. It takes all the patience and perseverance of their admirers to survive these assault courses. Small wonder that both buyers and press are turning, in steadily increasing numbers, back to the wit and appeal of the French.

If we were talking about Paris at the top, couture level then Yves St Laurent would still be king, but in the ready-to-wear, once again the year has been dominated by Karl Lagerfeld.

At the beginning of the year he was working, reluctantly it seemed, under the Chloé banner. There was already open talk of a rift and it seemed an omen that the theme of Lagerfeld's collection was a tribute to his seamstresses. It seemed to be his way of saying goodbye and thank you to them even if he couldn't wait to go. His necklaces were cotton reels and scissors, his bracelets pincushions, complete with multi-coloured pins.

By the time the autumn shows had come around there was a new label on the Paris scene. Karl Lagerfeld was on his own, or at least the name was, thanks to the backing of the highly successful Maurice Biderman. The Biderman empire was established through the St Laurent menswear – ironic since there is practically open warfare between the two designers. The kind of remark Lagerfeld has been tossing around would, in previous centuries, have led to a meeting at dawn, with swords or pistols.

● KARL LAGERFELD FOR CHLOE

● KARL LAGERFELD

● JEAN PATOU

● GIVENCHY

● KARL LAGERFELD FOR CHLOE

The first Lagerfeld collection was a qualified success. The American buyers loved it, yet somehow the Lagerfeld magic was slightly under par. The second will be better, when Karl has settled into his new home.

Meanwhile, there was plenty to applaud in a collection which from anyone else would have rated as tops. He has a new way of layering cloth, which he describes as "mille feuille", which gives movement and femininity to navy georgette dresses. His trousers (an essential part of winter 84) are narrow at the hip, ultra wide at the ankle, under cropped, fan seamed jackets. His shift dresses in jersey have equally flaring sleeves and taper to the knee from wide padded shoulders. For evening, narrow columns of navy georgette, with "mille feuille" panels, are worn over flaring trousers in the same fabric and have just wide ebony and ivory bangles as decoration.

Alongside his own collection Lagerfeld has continued to design for Chanel, both couture and ready-to-wear. While outsiders question his staying power, with all this work plus extras like the Fendi furs in Italy, his own staff have no qualms. "He has so much talent he could design a dozen collections," says one of his young assistants. Certainly he has had a remarkable success with Chanel. His predecessor, Philippe Guibourge (previously with Dior) designed beautiful Chanel ready-to-wear yet it did not move ahead with any speed.

Lagerfeld has achieved something quite remarkable. The clothes still say Chanel. They could not come from any other house. Yet at the same time they have become Lagerfeld's Chanel. Perhaps the success has come because he has had the sense to move away from what had become almost a caricature of the suit, all braid and wishy-washy tweed. His best Chanels are those in navy jersey, still with all the gold buttons but with the true Chanel chic.

Even Madame Chanel, despite herself, would have approved of clothes like the black jersey tunic, pockets low on the hip, over an ankle length skirt with deep, inverted pleat. The crisp white collar and turn back cuffs, the black ribbon bow and the gold and jewelled chains are pure Chanel. What is missing from Lagerfeld's highly successful life is a couture collection under his own name, something which may count for a lot to him. Perhaps this will be next year's news.

Meanwhile, at Chloé they have been reeling from the blow of his absence. Anyone following on had an impossible task. The sacrificial lamb was Guy Paulin, a much adored man and an excellent sportswear designer. If he is ever allowed to make his own way through the minefield there is no doubt Chloé would once again have a fine, though different, collection.

At first glance his initial offering was mixed and showed signs of suffering from too many cooks taking a hand. Nevertheless, there are hopeful indications, like the cinnamon brown teddy cloth jackets and oatmeal wrap-over suits, and the knubbly tweed long cardigan over high collared little yellow sweater and pale apricot easy crêpe trousers. Paulin has an unusual colour sense, subtle and pretty, plus a sure hand with separates which could be used to advantage if the Chloé folk will allow him to flourish.

The year had started with a question mark over the Paris-based designers and their future, with the Japanese arriving in force and the Italians taking away a large slice of even the French home market.

What transpired in the spring collections, and emerged still more in the autumn, was that the questions

● JEAN-PAUL GAULTIER

● CLAUDE MONTANA

● ANGELO TARLAZZI

● CLAUDE MONTANA

● THIERRY MUGLER

really applied to the Japanese. While Rei Kawakubo of Comme des Garçons had set off in new directions, her aggressively feminist approach, relevant and influential in her own country, had a limited role to play in Europe. Her models still had unkempt hair, bruised make-up, her clothes still wrapped and tied, albeit with some elegance. She appeared to be standing still.

Of the rest of the Tokyo group, the designer that stood out at the beginning of the year and consolidated his position six months later was Yohji Yamomoto. His floor length duster coats in clear colours and narrow skirts with high foldover waistbands for spring heralded a more easily assimilated style, an impression strengthened by his autumn collection. His sweaters, in chocolate and ox-blood red, in linen and wool knitted on large needles, mixed plain with marled yarn sections to give a patchwork effect, and were among the best in Paris. He has a Miyake-like inventiveness with fabric, rolling up the collars of his coats like tubes, stiffening scarves so that they stand away from the body. His extra-long cardigans in satin over body-hugging lambswool sweater dresses in shades of geranium confirmed that the Japanese designers are making their way towards a more feminine, colourful, sexy approach.

Yohji Yamomoto seems set to be a permanent member of the international designer group but the major Japanese name is still without doubt Issey Miyake. Putting into words what makes any designer great is always difficult but with Miyake it is virtually impossible. How can anyone explain why the way he folds fabric can be so beautiful it brings a tear to your eye? He can even make a raincoat irresistible like his spring ones in anthracite grey, ending well below the calf, with waistlength yokes that hang in folds over the tentlike coats. He uses the best of the Japanese shapes but takes them beyond the ethnic and into high fashion, like the sweaters with the deep kimono sleeves rolled up to the shoulders, Obi sashed over side draped skirts.

His superb sense of theatre was at its best with his autumn collection. Masks in gold or soft blue were modelled on the faces of the girls wearing them, adding drama to the hessian weave duffle coats and hip-wrapped side striped wool skirts that reached ankle length. His ridge knit cardigans are extended into a scarf end with an extra armhole to be folded around for extra warmth.

For many years Issey Miyake was almost a cult figure, much admired by his followers, unknown to many others. His compatriot Kenzo attracted a wider audience.

Although Japanese, Kenzo has never reflected his origins in his designs. Like Miyake, he has never sought to cling to a Japanese label but sees himself as having an international approach. Youth and dash were his trademarks rather than Oriental mysticism, though the recent taste for all things Japanese has tempted him into designing the occasional kimono-inspired coat. For the spring 84 collections he basked in the unaccustomed security of a fresh backer and celebrated by spending a sizeable slice of his new-found cash on a spectacular show. The setting was a striking château just outside Paris, the attractions enhanced by floodlighting, a casino and the struggle to get a ticket to get in to see the fun.

On a giant staircase the models showed a collection of charming and easy to wear blue and white or pink and white striped calico smocks, waist cropped jackets, bunchy skirts and narrow trousers. Towards late

- THIERRY MUGLER

- SONIA RYKIEL

- THIERRY MUGLER

- JEAN PATOU

- YVES ST LAURENT

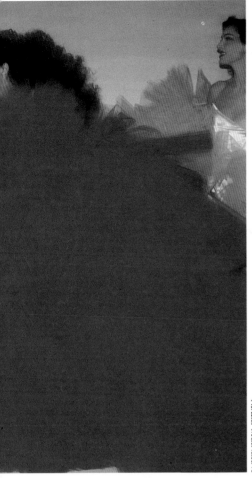

evening the stage was filled with these same shapes but in glorious gold or silver tissue and the gardens outside exploded with fireworks. A stunning occasion that displayed that Parisian confidence to perfection. For autumn it was back to the more usual runway and suits with giant-width trousers and short man-styled jackets or bathrobes (seen all over Paris, sometimes in Noel Coward Paisleys) with collars and ties. His ever present peasants wore for autumn multi-coloured boleros and sweaters over, of all things, tartan skirts.

Talk of spectacular leads inevitably to Claude Montana, who has been presenting us with astounding displays for several years without ever, it seems, repeating himself or running out of ideas.

In the spring collection his themes included colonial uniforms of several kinds, from a romantic view of the Raj, (all beribboned epaulettes and multi-pocketed jackets over puttee-cuffed pleated trousers) to uniforms for the Heads of Emergent States, naughtily covered with bejewelled decorations. As Montana designs for a leading leather manufacturer there are always exciting leathers in his collections. For spring they were zipped with diamanté, for autumn big shouldered, full backed jackets in purple or grass green.

Winter pastels are another Montana favourite, and for 84 he used pale sand cashmeres and gabardines for flare-backed coats, with wider shoulders than ever, and rib knit sleeves. Yet he brought welcome colour with his oversized jackets in turquoise, shocking pink or violet wool velours over black velvet tights.

A measure of his showmanship was one scene which stopped the show yet was in fact just a group of twinsets in cashmere over molebrown whipcord jodhpurs and riding boots. They were

in gorgeous colours but they were just twinsets. What Claude Montana understands is how to present wearable clothes with drama and impact.

Nevertheless, when it comes to spectaculars it is hard to beat the major jokers in Paris, Jean Paul Gaultier and Thierry Mugler.

Gaultier started the year by taking the colonial look, with its epaulettes and flap pockets and adding a fez plus army socks and running shoes. By autumn he had moved into tartans in a big way, for vast trousers and velvet collared overcoats. An occasional short, tight waistcoat is worn over wrapped hips and check trousers. Knitted polo shirts are as long as dresses and have shirt tails that wrap around the hip.

Gaultier shows are a succession of jokes but always they are based on current themes and underneath the crazy accessories there are perfectly wearable clothes. Mugler saves his more practical ideas for the collections he produces for wholesale manufacture. For his shows he blends wit with innovation so that in one and the same collection there are tightly wrapped housedresses in gaudy coloured nylon and stiffened faille strapless tutus over narrow trousers yet there are also interesting jersey dresses in two tones like cut away shouldered swimsuits with contrast skirts. Above all he gave a new look to denim, with swirling skirted Sixties style dresses.

When it came to the autumn collection Mugler took his addiction to the spectacular to its logical conclusion. He hired from the city of Paris a vast stadium, sold 4,000 tickets to the public, invited 2,000 press and buyers and presented a collection that amused some, offended others, bored nobody.

There were many ski outfits in jersey, practical, with interesting

- CHLOE
- CHLOE
- SONIA RYKIEL
- GIVENCHY

detail. Hooded burnous dresses in pastel wool satin flattered, tight suits with low gored skirts in bouclé did not.

Mugler's enthusiasm for the theatre came with the late-day clothes. We had seen nuns and listened to the Hallelujah Chorus a few times during the autumn shows but religion really hit Mugler. He presented us with golden winged angels in purple satin, the Angel Gabriel in pleated gold lamé and, finally, a Madonna descending from the roof and looking suspiciously like model Pat Cleveland.

Spectaculars are fun and effective in the right hands but there are times when the clothes become submerged in all the drama. Small wonder that some designers feel their ideas would be better expressed in their own salons. Designers like Sonia Rykiel, for example, whose intimate, understated clothes, with their subtle sex appeal, have always looked best in her own surroundings. Only the fact that her insurance brokers grew pale at the thought of a thousand or so buyers and press pouring into her shop persuaded her into the show tents.

She may not have liked the idea but she has managed to evolve a highly effective way of showing her collection on a large scale yet maintaining her very individual style. It is simple and relies on a few special items, like the sweaters with their diamanté slogans, and the accessories, like the felt bowlers and the thin brown cigars. For the rest, for 1984 the Rykiel look is long and lean with side fastening coats and skinny jersey dresses. Her colours are clear pinks, vivid and soft blues, an unabashed red as well as grey, brown and, of course, black.

The shadow of Balenciaga hovered over the year. Both Givenchy and Yves St Laurent showed sculptured shift dresses, and the new ready-to-wear designer at Gerard Penneroux (previously with Dior Menswear) devoted half his collections to melon-shouldered uncluttered two piece suits and dresses in the Balenciaga mould.

Despite his training under the Spanish master, Ungaro continues to move in quite another direction, with his ultra sexy "businessman's afternoon" clothes.

Another ex-Dior man, Guy Douvier, works with the house of Guy Laroche, where in previous years there has been more than a touch of the poule de luxe. Today, although sex appeal is never disregarded, the collection is fresh, unexaggerated and very pleasing. His olive and navy tartan blazers, with soft wide shoulders, velvet half collar, over sunray-pleated wool crêpe skirts and white shirts with shining satin ribbon bows looked good. I agreed with my American journalist neighbour that we were looking at clothes at least as good as 90 per cent of the rest yet where were all the crowds, the ballyhoo?

It was the same at Angelo Tarlazzi. His long lambswool tunics bound all around the hips with contrasting jersey over a further skirt, again in lambswool, were terrific. A narrow length belt worn just about at thigh level accentuated the curvy silhouette. His big shouldered leather jackets are cropped at the waist and ruched, then worn over another basque of matching leather, buttoned over wrapover jersey skirts. As befits an Italian, his colours are superb, violet with grass green and fuchsia; ice pink, shocking pink and orange (a combination of hot colours seen frequently during the autumn shows).

It is at these less frenetic shows that the message of Paris comes through loud and clear. Where else can we see so much talent, handled so professionally?

● CLAUDE MONTANA

THE MILAN COLLECTIONS

Brenda Polan

● Italian style, in the second half of the Twentieth Century, is without doubt the most mature expression of humanity's need to reconcile its aesthetic yearnings with all the practical considerations which shape the rooms it lives in, the tools it uses and the clothes it wears. The society which has spawned this style is unequal, economically chaotic and politically immature. Casual, open, institutionalised corruption prevails as in no other Western society. Poverty and the exploitation of labour both thrive in the next street to opulent displays of wealth and consumerism at its most elitist.

It cannot be an accident. Think of Harry Lime's reflection on Switzerland: "They had brotherly love, five hundred years of democracy and peace, and what is that nation's most significant contribution to international culture? The cuckoo clock."

So, when the world's fashion press and store buyers arrived in Milan to see the ready-to-wear collections for spring and summer 1984, only the neophytes were startled by the paradox which awaited them. The newspapers and the television screens were lurid with pictures of distraught, grief-stricken men, women and children made homeless by not altogether unexpected earth tremors in Pozzuoli in the south of the country. The local bureaucrats, short on resources, competence and any aid from the government, were filmed and photographed as they closed their ears to the pleas and then the anger of the victims, shrugged helplessly and retreated behind their office doors.

Up north in Milan the designer shows were also discovered to be homeless, displaced from their usual venue by a machine-tool exhibition. Within 48 hours the cavernous, hangar-like space of an unusued pavilion at the Fiera de Milano had been carved into four gigantic show halls with runway, cabine, carpets, sophisticated lighting system and seating for thousands. Two dozen private showrooms for exhibiting companies, press rooms, banks, telex,

NIALL MCINERNY

● GIANNI VERSACE

telephones, lavatories, two refreshment bars and two restaurants, a flower shop, bookstall and a beauty parlour had all been installed.

To a certain extent the contrast is that between north and south. To a greater extent it is that between the profitable and the unprofitable. Italy's designers make money and, fuelled by glamour borrowed from the top designers showing twice a year in Milan, so does the rest of the manufacturing industry which is fashion-based.

So in Italy the names of the top designers – Giorgio Armani, Gianni Versace, Gianfranco Ferre, Luciano Soprani – are as well known to the general public as the names of movie stars, opera divas (to which class of person many bear a strong resemblance) and football heros. But if any grouping of designers ever earned its palazzos, villas, yachts, bodyguards and fawning acolytes, it is this one. There are, at the top of Italian fashion, no overnight successes destined to fade and go bankrupt in one or two seasons. The Italian industry is a canny one, well supported by government and fabric manufacturers, which takes only the most calculated of risks.

This means that it still has a system in which young designers can serve an apprenticeship, learning and perfecting the techniques of their profession in large design studios. It means that by the time a designer is in a position of any prominence, he or she has a mature approach to their work, a consistent vision and a controlled imagination. And that means an essentially commercial, rationalised attitude to their work and a belief in the steady development of ideas rather than seasonal changes of tack.

Gianni Versace, whose experiments with fabric, particularly metallic ones, have advanced textile technology, speaks for the majority when he says: "My ambition is to give women a

● MONTANA FOR COMPLICE

● VERSACE

● MARIO VALENTINO

wardrobe which works in the way a man's does. There cannot be sudden change every season so that everything else in the wardrobe looks out of date. Women should be able, like men, to add something fresh and beautiful each season, something which extends the possibilities of their wardrobe without cancelling the usefulness of the rest of it."

Though that may be the philosophy of all the important designers, they differ on the details. Versace himself frowns fiercely and continues: "But that does not mean dressing women in men's clothes. I try to understand the woman of today, her life, her needs, her desires, and I try to make clothes which express her spirit, her sense of being. And that is different from a man's."

And, indeed, in the two collections he designed for 1984, he could be seen developing his own extremely feminine version of what we have come to recognise as Italian classics. Relying heavily on luxurious fabrics, this style of dress is basically simple but utilises accessories to update itself and lend a touch of wit. Italian clothes are rarely fun; they are not exuberant enough. But they sometimes, as with the animal motif sweaters of Mariucca Mandelli-Pinto of Krizia, have a sophisticated lightheartedness which docs just as well.

In Versace's work this is more and more showing itself in the bold use of contrasting colours, body-hugging, curvacious silhouettes beneath the broad but rounded shoulders which

● GIORGIO ARMANI

● BYBLOS

● GIORGIO ARMANI

the Italians love so much, and ever more sensuous fabrics handled in an almost disrespectful way. He manages to imply both opulence and youthfulness at the same time.

If, in 1984, Versace liked the idea if not the substance, of a man's wardrobe for a woman, Giorgio Armani was inspired by both. This designer is preoccupied with refining both the extent and the content of women's wardrobes and external influences and his own exploration of the possibilities of refinement took him towards menswear. His spring collections for his own label and for Erreuno, strongly menswear-influenced, pointed to the path most designers were to take, to a larger or smaller degree, in their autumn collections.

In fact, in October 1983, when Armani showed his collection for the following spring, he decided at the eleventh hour, to make his move towards androgynous dressing more emphatic and substituted many of his original designs with outfits from his menswear collection. Press and buyers, recognising that Armani had got it right, applauded frantically.

By the following March, menswear was all-pervading. Again and again designers sent battalions of models out into the glare of the lights dressed as men. Their hatless (except for some schematic workingmen's caps) heads were short-back-and-sided and slicked down like the painted hair on a 1920s tailor's dummy or sculpted into the neatest of jaw-level bobs. Make-up was minimal, lips and

cheeks unrouged, eyes subtly emphasised.

With few exceptions the models were shod in clumpy lace-up brogues or well-polished riding boots. And the bodies in between these two impeccably minimalist extremities came clad in an assortment of male attire. There were pinstripe city suits, sometimes with shirt and tie, sometimes with a soft, unadorned buttoned-up shirt or simple round-neck cashmere sweater. There were unstructured tweed sports jackets teamed with matching or contrasting wide-legged tweed trousers or ubiquitous grey flannels. Most coats were voluminous herringbone or Donegal tweed greatcoats; the rest were melton or camel hair gentlemen's city coats, a broad-shouldered version of the college coat which has been popular for some seasons, or extra-roomy gabardine trenchcoats.

There were larger than life cricket cardigans worn with cream flannel pants, straight-legged and turn-upped, and chunky, cable-knit sweaters worn with men's mufflers loosely knotted in front. There were many uniform-style jackets, a development of the mess-dress look which was strong for spring and summer both in Italy and Paris and which the American designer, Ralph Lauren, had favoured in a hybrid military/safari look for spring. These, epauletted, braided and sometimes be-medalled, were worn with jodhpurs or riding skirts.

Further down the social scale, the

workman's voluminous all-in-one made a come-back, often unwaisted and starkly simple. Occasionally a swirling coachman's cape replaced the greatcoat and the tweed suits sometimes took on a spivvy, back streets of Naples air with outrageously wide shoulders, draped back and tapering, below the hip length. These once or twice became loudly plaid and rather Max Wall to match the Crazy Gang two-for-the-price-of-one fake fur (sometimes real) overcoats.

As was to be expected, the androgynous look was strongest at Armani. However, for those women unhappy at the prospect at trousers, trousers and more trousers, he had included a short, sharp skirt, gathered into a low-slung waistband and narrowing to its on-the-knee hem, and two lengths of wrap-around sarong-style skirt, knee-length and just above ankle-length.

This sarong-shape skirt resembled Versace's recurring tulip-shape and was destined, as the American collections a month later proved, to be influential. Unlike Versace, Armani remained in the sombre corner of the palette: neutral greys, beiges, browns, blacks, indigo. But the tweeds and the prints on the skirts were, nevertheless, richer and more complex than most well-bred chaps would care for.

At Erreuno too, where Armani did not appear to acknowledge the audience's applause but where his signature was obvious, the look departed from menswear only long enough to substitute either a short pencil skirt or a long, narrow skirt for the trousers.

● MISSONI

● VERSACE

● MISSONI

32

Here, however, patterns departed even further from acceptable menswear although fabrics and colours were just as sombre. The one bright colour was hunting pink – quite suitable for a gentleman.

The rest of Milan's elite corps of designers worked somewhere in the middle ground between Armani's commitment to androgyny and Versace's to feminity. Here were many of the garments we have learned to regard as unisex and which, in one form or another, are an indispensable part of the modern person's wardrobe. Gianfranco Ferre went into spring with a look which placed great emphasis on the hipline and although this was softened for autumn, his comfortably large blousons retained that outline. The blouson featured in a more structured version in stamped chocolate leather in Gianni Versace's first suede and leather collection for Mario Valentino and in luxurious fur in Karl Lagerfeld's Fendi collection.

Keith Varty, designing for Byblos, produced sporty duffle coats and jackets which he showed over ankle-freezing drainpipe trousers. Mariucca Mandelli at Krizia showed strictly tailored hacking gear in various permutations so black, navy and dark brown.

Most designers showed some kind of outfit for evening based on what the Americans call the tuxedo and the French le smoking and several had moved on to what the British call a smoking jacket – a classically cut, lapelled jacket in dark velvet with a

- KARL LAGERFELD FOR FENDI

- GINAFRANCO FERRE

- FENDI

dressing-gown cord to secure it.

Androgyny is a fashion mood which came up from the street where it reflected a desire, both mischievous and seriously iconoclastic, on the part of young men and women, to explore the possibilities of gender confusion. Street fashion is a British phenomenon and although it is closely watched by the more alert of the great international designers, it is chiefly disseminated through pop groups, their on and off-stage dress and their videos. The international menswear collections are showing the effects of Boy George's floral frocks only in looser shapes and louder patterns, but womenswear, ever more sensitive, is marching, in autumn 1984, to Annie Lennox's androgynous drum.

In Milan, however, it was the designers who had absorbed the influence, pondered upon it, and then merely exploited it as a leitmotiv whose credibility was the greater. That, after all, is the traditional Italian way. Italian style is averse to extremes; its great attraction is its lack of gimmickry, its maturity and restraint. Versace himself used the masculine coats and jackets to emphasise the slender, sensuous proportions of the clinging dresses, narrow skirts and soft wrap tops whose curved lines echoed and were more sympathetic to the planes of the female body.

Similarly, Luciano Soprani, in his own collection and in the one he designs for Basile, did his greatcoats in mouthwatering shades of cream bearing a shadow plaid of apple, beige

or grey and the spiv's jacket in Irish-mist Donegal. Under them he put lean, soft angora jersey dresses or long, swirling wool crepe skirts. Another coat eschewed the severity of lapels in favour of an attached toga-effect scarf.

Gianfranco Ferre allowed the lapels of his man-shaped tweed jacket to grow into trailing scarf-ends which were loosely knotted, muffler-like, just above waist level. He also had long, easy skirts and pretty, feminine sweaters in soft angora. He trimmed huge navy quilted coats with dark brown beaver, Italy's favourite fur trim, and layered a short, shift-shape pinafore dress over a cream silk shirt then piled a slightly longer, full gilet on top and a long trenchcoat on top of that, all in the same soft beige worsted.

Karl Lagerfeld's collection for Fendi was, except for the preponderance of trousers and menswear fabrics, sensuously and dramatically feminine. The Fendi spring collection had been less successful with a strangely obsessive theme of aprons over everything and some strikingly unattractive print frocks. The winter collection was, as ever, a triumph. The furs, suedes and leathers ranged from aggressively sporty to demurely romantic in the style of a turn-of-the-century heroine and coloured in all the shades of brown from the most delicate mushroom through rich rusts and chestnuts to tobacco and bitter chocolate.

At Krizia, Mariucca Mandelli

developed her hard-shouldered line of spring into a sharp-looking point for autumn and presented some of the most strictly tailored redingotes and college coats in Milan. But hers were essentially feminine collections, controlled, modern and youthful with that sense of fun so rare in the work of her compatriots.

And although his dimensions were, characteristically, much more generous, the same was true of both Claude Montana's 1984 collections for Complice. This was the year when Montana left behind all the fancy dress elements, all the theatrical posturing which had marred some of his earlier work. His delight in uniforms and active sportswear was still there but strongly controlled and brilliantly executed. Most memorable for spring was his mess dress and for autumn his more businesslike military, layered look, his softly linear 1910 lady cricketer look and his *Raiders of the Lost Ark* adventures in softly wrapped red suede top, black suede jodhpurs and wickedly polished black riding boots.

Montana is always more disciplined, more commercial in the work he does for the Italian house of Complice and it is likely that this discipline is now shaping the work he does in Paris. If that is so then there is much to be said for Italy's strange, paradoxical nature – at once cynical and sensitive, heartless and emotional, irrational and calculating, chaotically self-destructive and unequalled in its disciplined, intensely professional creativity.

● COMPLICE

THE
NEW YORK
COLLECTIONS
Lorna Koski

● As the Hammerstein/Kern classic goes, "Fish gotta swim, birds gotta fly," and the spring New York collections, which got underway in one of the most optimistic retail climates in recent seasons, featured a number of the major American designers doing what comes most naturally. But as a veteran fashion observer once remarked, "the test of a real designer is that when you go up and look at what he's doing at the start of any season, you never know what you're going to see".

And accordingly, several of New York's major designers created good spring collections by ringing a variety of surprising changes on what they're known to be best at ... while others who were less successful are showing signs of becoming permanently mired in the limiting dimensions of what's known as a signature style.

While the overall effect of this was to create what was, to say the least, a highly diverse season, there were a few unifying themes. There was a cleaning-up and simplifying which gave a breath of fresh air to a range of collections ranging from Oscar de la Renta's European-flavored looks which, for the first time, were minus full-blown ballgowns, to Calvin Klein's, which overwhelmingly espoused a minimalist, lean-lined simplicity. The other key message was the importance of the dress, which owed its prominence, in part, to the earlier, chemise-dominated European collections, but which was interpreted on New York's Seventh Avenue in versions from sexy, hip-draped silks to easy, eminently business like trenchcoat-dresses.

A third theme in the spring collections was length – both brief and very long for day. Retailers have been claiming for years that length is no longer an issue, and that the same women will wear short or long dresses, depending on the shape, material or mood of the look. But the clothes are actually intended for two different customers. Those whose ladies favor Parisian-style clothes –

short, snappy and vividly colored – voted in favor of leg-baring lengths for day, and others advocated an ankle-skimming sweep of skirts.

The season also featured the return of the duster, or warm-weather coat. These lightweight layers appeared in many collections in versions from oversized linen trenchcoats to full-cut versions in snowy wool, and in view of 1984's unpredictable spring weather throughout much of the country, were very timely.

With his spring collection, Calvin Klein came full circle from what had been one of the most surprising about-faces in recent American fashion history. One year before, Klein, who, up until then, had been known as a prime exponent of easy sportswear, went breathlessly urbane with an overtly sexy, ultra-fitted and super-sophisticated collection which was as European in silhouette and feeling as his previous clothes had been All-American. For spring 1984, Klein went back to nature with a fluid and easy collection glorifying the American girl – specifically a long-limbed tanned beauty with fresh-scrubbed good looks that were in little need of cosmetic aid. His collection showcased her long, slender body in apparently artless long skirts and shirts, narrow, ankle-skimming cash-mere sundresses, and simple linen dresses – most of them in exaggerat-edly long lengths from lower-calf to mid-ankle.

And while Calvin Klein was attiring his American beauty in simple clothes

which would suit her for his favored sophisticated, but dressed-down retreats: Fire Island or Santa Fe, New Mexico, cosmopolite Oscar de la Renta was dressing the luncheon set from New York to Rio in continental-flavored looks which, while more restrained than those he usually shows, certainly didn't lack for flash. Among the hits of his collection were the hip-conscious chemises in silk and cashmere, vivid mixed print looks combining tropical florals and stripes, and, needless to say, sensual evening looks, from a one-shoulder silk siren dress with a single rhinestone strap to shapely satin evening jackets orna-mented with embroidered parrots over long, slim skirts.

While others are urbane world trav-ellers, Ralph Lauren and Perry Ellis are Time Bandits – raiding lost – but rarely far-removed eras of culture and fashion for often highly-successful inspiration. Few of Ralph Lauren's multitudinous fans, who ravenously devour his collections and the offer-ings of his various licensees, are ever likely to enquire as to what his message is, since he makes it perfectly clear. And his public is with him all the way, whether he takes them to the American frontier, as he has in the past, or, as he did this season, to the African veldt. Everything he does is carefully presented, with a highly-styl-ized eye to authenticity – and if it isn't always original, then it isn't meant to be. But watching a deeply tanned fiftyish woman buy one of Lauren's Victorian ingenue camisoles and skirts for herself (a look that would be perfect for a very young girl) shows that he has certainly tapped into an unexpected lode of fantasy in the American subconscious.

And while older women would probably look considerably better in something more sophisticated, Lauren's clothes always look their hard-to-resist best on the unadorned WASP beauties he favors to show his collections, whose cool good looks are reminiscent of the prettiest of the county girls who people *Jennifer's Diary*. For spring, perpetual Anglophile Lauren took his audience on an African safari to the vanished colonial world of the Thirties, as it was created in the movies – not the hardbitten *African Queen* but the alternating cool and sultry *Mogambo*. His silhouettes ranged from safari jackets, classic pants and trenchcoats executed in linen or lightweight silk tweeds, to aristocratic ingenue looks like a linen Norfolk jacket and long, slim skirt shown with the Claudine-like touch of a black-bowed white blouse. He also created slender, unflappable white linen suits with long, narrow skirts which would be perfect for presiding over an elaborate tea in a now-vanished colonial outpost.

Perry Ellis said the inspiration for his spring collection was Australia, but the clothes he showed suggested the champagne sophistication of *Private Lives* more than the rugged outback of *The Chant of Jimmy Blacksmith*. Perhaps he was thinking of the flappers of Doris Lessing's Down Under in the *Martha Quest* novels. But regardless of their theoretical origin, many of the clothes he showed succeeded on their own terms in a spring collection which, if less strong than that of the previous fall, was still full of grown up and distinctive looks. Ellis, a great advocate of wit and whimsy, restrained his elfin side this time to good effect in well-cut dresses, from all-white pleated tennis looks with the ease of gymslips to his long navy middy dresses and urbane satin linen dresses shown with slightly shorter dusters. He also provided good-looking haberdashery trouser suits, and, as a designer who made his name with knits, handsome V-front sweater vests over ultra-long pleated skirts.

Bill Blass who, along with Oscar de la Renta, dresses the leading ladies of the luncheon and charity set – and, not incidentally, some of the country's wealthiest women – indefatigably trav-

NIALL MCINERNY

NIALL MCINERNY

erses the whole of the United States with his rich clothes. And he knows what women all over the country want: a certain sumptuousness and luxury, and he was undeterred by the restrained mood that permeated much of Seventh Avenue spring. He gave his ladies what they like in cleverly draped, checked and spotted silk dresses, mixed print suits, and graphic chemises – shown with sassy little veiled hats – and, of course, extravagant evening looks. But though Blass is big in Oklahoma, he lives in New York and Connecticut, and has a thorough sense of how to combine urbane dressed up and dressed down elements – as in his simple coatdresses or the cropped evening trenchcoat shown over a slim, long dress and a vibrant fuchsia one-shoulder crepe column that was among the most striking night looks of the season.

Anne Klein, which has been designed for years by the team of Donna Karan and Louis Dell'Olio, had one of its less successful spring collections, straying from the teams – and the firm's – traditional strength, pure-lined American sportswear, into uncertain territory. While some of the day looks were handsome – the over-sized linen polo coats, for example – evening was curiously tarty, in pastel loungewear or 42nd Street sequins.

The big news at Norma Kamali, apart from her all-concrete OMO boutique, which opened in the last month of 1983, was her new ladylike daytime looks and ultra-glamorous, vampish evening entrancemakers, both in utterly different moods from the street-smart sweats that made her name. The day looks were proper "ensembles", as they used to be known, featuring broadshouldered coats in black and white printed rayon over very feminine matching long skirts or dresses. And her lamé siren dresses recalled the most extravagant excesses of Travis Banton for Marlene Dietrich – with long, narrow torsos spilling seductively into exaggerated fishtail skirts.

Mary McFadden and Michaele

● CALVIN KLEIN

● STEPHEN SPROUSE

● STEPHEN SPROUSE

● OSCAR DE LA RENTA

Vollbracht also had plenty of fantasy. McFadden's was mainly in her unlikely program notes – which stated that the collection was dedicated to Lorenzo di Medici and – while many of the looks were anything but Renaissance, what was best was her signature pure-lined pleated looks; while Vollbracht presented a lineup of his pictorial printed looks, which are such favorites with the Hollywood set – in motifs from bright balloons to Noh masks. And while Halston, the dominating figure of late-Seventies American fashion, seemed to be putting forth most of his considerable creative energy into his multi-million dollar collection for the giant chain, J C Penney's, he gave his spring collection considerably less definition. Many of the looks lacked the linear purity he has been known for, except for renditions of familiar tailored looks such as his one-lapel suit.

For some time, New York's fashion press, retailers, and bright young things – and in many cases, these are three mutually exclusive groups – had been asking where the new young talents were. And while the New York streets and boites may not be as densely populated with wildly dressed and coiffed young things as, say, London, there are still plenty of fanatical fashion freaks here who live for clothes. They have long felt that things were simply too boring and out-of-touch in what they consider the excessively safe and cash-conscious world of Seventh Avenue. But many of them found someone they could admire in the person of thirtyish designer Stephen Sprouse, who had shown his first small group of clothes only a year before.

Sprouse, a long-time devotee of the world-within-worlds of rock music, after-hours clubs, and fashion, who had been a sometime silk screener, photographer and couturier to singer Debbie Harry, entwined his passion for the Sixties with an exact sense of what the jaded late-night world is all about in a series of lively and surprising spring clothes, from spare little minidresses to precisely tailored coats based on men's jackets.

A few stores sampled his graffiti-painted sequins, motorcycle-gang leathers, and neon-colored suits last fall, and found, often to their surprise, that they sold. And within a short time, this designer, a perfectionist devotee of what was known in his favorite era as "the total look", became one of the most talked-about

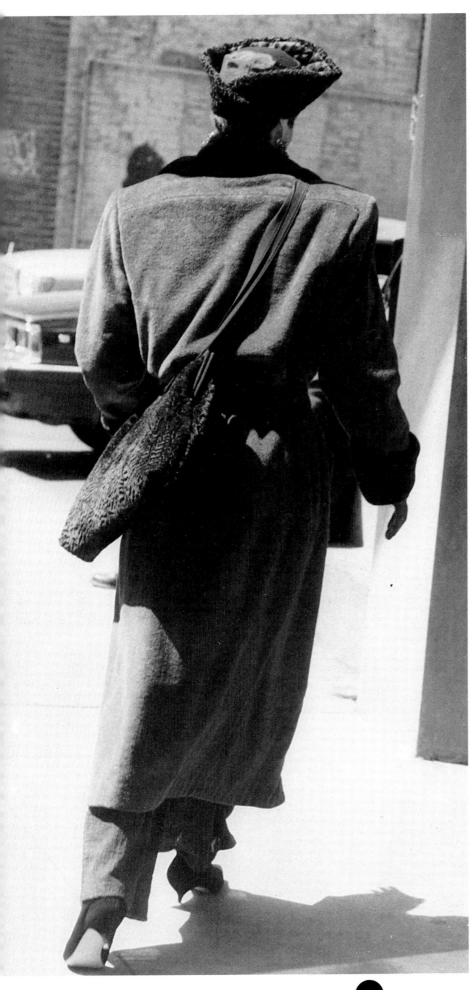

designers on Seventh Avenue. Stores across the country started to Sprouse up with everything from his vivid trapeze dresses to graffiti-patterned tights and silver jewelry spelling out "Peace" and "1984". And Sprouse had his most direct influence by reintroducing to the eye – and then the palette – of many his wildly vibrant colors, those lime-green and acid-orange shades known in the Swinging Sixties as Day-glos.

The essence of fashion, is, of course, change, and the fall collections ushered in a new mood in New York. The season's key – and at times, overwhelming – messages were haberdashery-inspired looks and the revival of vibrant color, and both themes often registered in a single silhouette. The menswear looks were given impetus by Paris's and Milan's masculine-feminine fall collections, which were filled to overflowing with handsome coats, many varieties of full-cut pants, smoking robes and, needless to say, mannish accessories: from sensible shoes to pocket handkerchiefs and men's ties. Versions of these looks permeated American fall, often felicitously, since sportswear is many New York designers' strong suit, but at times a tad alarmingly, in butch and bulky layers or groups of sporty silhouettes so similar that it was difficult to tell one designer's work from another's.

And while the plethora of menswear looks had fashion writers leafing desperately through their *Thesauruses* to come up with more synonyms for "man-styled" (Saville Row-inspired, boyish, man-tailored, mannish, masculine-feminine, and, of course, what quickly became the most overused word in the fashion language: androgynous), there were also other key elements in the New York collections. The color revival owed a great deal to Yves Saint Laurent's, Claude Montana's and Valentino's vivid use of it, and also to the more strident palette of London designers such as Vivienne Westwood and, in New York, Stephen Sprouse. While the color was abundantly

● FEZZA

● NORMA KAMALI

welcome, to replace the plethora of black which has darkened New York's day and evening landscape for far too long, the revival of winter white also was a desirable palette change. Sweater looks continued to be important, and several key New York designers created some strong looks for evening.

Ralph Lauren was one of the most successful advocates of the haberdashery look this season, and with his fondness for British tailored classics, the look was a natural for him. Translated into the American, his versions recall the ineffable WASP style of such Anglo-Saxon enclaves as Southampton, Newport and Bucks County, Pennsylvania. In a good coat season, Lauren's were among the handsomest, from his sporty navy cashmere coat shown over low-key separates to his one-button black evening coat with a Chesterfield collar. He also provided plenty of very English fabric mixes, as in a tweed jacket over a paisley challis skirt and muted plaid shirt or a herringbone jacket with a Fair Isle sweater and tweed pants. He did softly feminine dresses, too, such as the black ingenue dress with a white collar which was reminiscent of a French schoolgirl.

Calvin Klein also revisited his roots for fall in a collection of simple sportswear shapes reminiscent of the gimmick-free classics that made his name. Klein did good-looking coats, including polo versions, cardigan coats, balmacaans and trenches, in a range of fabrics from twill to herringbone tweeds. He, too, played with menswear fabrics, in layers of tailored separates in tweed over cashmere, flannel, or challis. Klein also scored with understated dresses, like his long black wool V-necks with the ease of a pullover over linen boatnecks, and his double-breasted wool gabardine or pinstriped flannel coatdresses. But his understated efforts worked less well at night, in a group of droopy-looking blouses and skirts.

Evening is, on the other hand, Oscar de la Renta's strong suit, and he did it, as always, with plenty of glitter and flashes of tropical color. Sensual De La Renta's rich nights start with long-stemmed and narrow silhouettes topped by slightly broader shoulders and with a sexy bareness at the throat or bosom. He did his Paris-inspired entrancemakers in black velvet with empire waists topped by beading, and in gold Lurex metallic with pleated skirts that were snug at

the hips and flared from the thighs to the floor. He also provided the intricate matador embroidery he's known for, on bright evening jackets and dress bodices, and did vivid versions of his signature rich peasants in blue, emerald green, magenta and scarlet silk.

But de la Renta is as ardent for day as for night, and even his suits are sexy and feminine, with bright nipped jackets under matching fuller-cut short coats over sleek, knee-length black skirts. And his short cashmere dresses are effortlessly seductive.

Equally effortless-seeming were Bill Blass's all-American daytime looks with big camel and pink double-faced wool coats over wide pants and jackets. In the same vein were his elegantly nonchalant long wool sweaters and twinsets, which for evening were pulled over full, flounced satin and or lace skirts, in red on red, pink on pink, and camel or gray over silver.

But many of Blass's evening looks were considerably more complicated, drenched in opulent embroidery, fur trim, or with lots of spiralling ruffles or second-skin draping. Still, that's what many of his wealthy ladies like, and there's little doubt that these bullion-displaying looks will be gracing galas and benefits for seasons to come, in American cities from Palm Beach to Palm Springs.

It's not as clear where Perry Ellis's customers will be wearing his fall looks. Ellis opened a time capsule this fall and suffused his collection with an atmosphere of nostalgia for 1920s Paris, which was frequently overwhelming if not actually stifling.

Mixed in among the cloche hats and massive numbers of knits and blouses and evening coats which he said were inspired by French artist, Sonia Delaunay, were skirts which went to the currently popular, Thirties-style, long lengths. These were often combined with Twenties boxiness in a single silhouette for an unfortunate droopiness. Some of the pairings, however, actually worked, showing Ellis's talent for carrying off the unlikely. Also successful were

● PERRY ELLIS

● BILL BLASS

some more straightforward sports-wear looks, such as a single-button checked pantsuit and his mannish sweater vests and pants.

And Perry Ellis, whether it's currently to his credit or not, is always distinctive, and sometimes is leader of the American pack. For fall, 1983, he had one of the handsomest and most innovatively proportioned collections in New York, and, while retailers and press alike disagreed violently on his current fall looks, with many disliking those derived from Miss Delaunay, there's no telling what he'll come up with next.

Donna Karan and Louis Dell'Olio put Anne Klein back on track with a strong fall collection featuring what they do best: fine sportswear tailoring in rich fabrics, rendered in a haber-dashery spirit. What distinguished their collection from many others, however, is that they know just how to handle these sporty looks which have been their traditional strength. They made a strong statement with classic coats, and with winter white, which showed up at its most striking in an alpaca coachman coat over pants and a huge, easy, white, cable knit pullover over matching wool pants.

Norma Kamali, however, did the unexpected for fall. Although, as always, she didn't show formally. She worked in denim, a fabric most desig-ners only take seriously in their cash-harvesting licensee collections. Kamali's versions of the fabric showed up in narrow pants topped by denim jackets and in her signature sexy gored skirts paired with red rayon skirts.

Her dramatically proportioned, broad-shouldered and nipped-waisted looks are a combination of thrift-shop elegance and street-smart wit which irresistibly suggests the style of SoHo and the East Village but her clothes will probably be all over American streets by autumn.

Stephen Sprouse had his first big formal show – although the word "formal" in connection with him is a contradiction in terms. In keeping with his fascination for rock music – and the tastes of many of his most ardent fans – Sprouse showed at the Ritz, a rock club in the East Village. While Bill Blass conducts his splend-idly orchestrated shows in the Pierre Hotel's Cotillion room, and Perry Ellis keeps to his own turf in his show-room, the choice of venue says a good deal about each designer. In Sprouse's case, the Ritz was great for

his fans, who filled its cavernous space to capacity, and less-thrilling for some retailers, who found the disorganized mob scene there less to their tastes.

Next to the show itself, which was either sensational or drastically over-staged, depending on one's point of view, the clothes paled a bit. The problem was that nearly all of them – the leather jackets, the graffiti sequins, the minidresses with cut-outs, the Day-glo suits – Sprouse had done before, so that the only surprise provided for some retailers was not what was on the runway, but the fact that they couldn't see it because they were locked out of the club after it filled up, by the overzealous Ritz gate-keepers. Still, the atmosphere was, as they used to say, a trip, and there's no denying Sprouse has had an impact. But while the world waits breathlessly for the return of the frug, it's up to him to make a new move.

Making some interesting moves of their own were a variety of other designers, who showed good collections in a frequently-weak fall season. Jackie Rogers, once Coco Chanel's favorite model, later a menswear retailer, and most recently, the owner of her own women's boutique on Madison Avenue, showed her first full collection, a felicitous blend of menswear looks and feminine slinkiness.

Her signature envelope chemises, tailored coatdresses, and her glam-orous evening slinks were all good-looking. Danny Noble, a young sports-wear designer from Philadelphia, made a strong statement with a small but lively collection including innova-tively proportioned Black Watch plaid looks, featuring cropped jackets over long turtlenecks and ankle-skimming pleated skirts.

Michael Kors, who's done well in recent seasons with his cashmeres, also did a confident fall collection. His best silhouette was a pale, shawl-collared tweed coat over man-tailored trousers, and he also created an inter-esting proportion with a simply draped dress under a cashmere coat and pants. And Catherine Hipp,

● NORMA KAMALI

● NORMA KAMALI

whose inventiveness sometimes gets the best of her, did some very handsome fall coats, full-cut with big collars or side-fastening with clipboard-style closings.

Robert Molnar had one of the season's most interesting collections. Molnar, who has been in the business for several years, first as a designer of a line of paper clothing and part-time club doorman, and, more recently, doing ready-to-wear under his own name, does styled-up clothing which blends Parisian-style allure with a cheeky American realism. For fall, Molnar's filmic show provided everything from bright, sexy knit dresses to bright-on-white Calder-inspired coats in silk screened wool. Some of his wilder looks, such as his velvet bras and silver lame pants, or his Nehru suits for women, are Sixties in feeling, but they have a thoroughly contemporary wit and a sexy body-consciousness that was rarer in a sportswear-dominated season.

After the two-and-a-half weeks of collections finished, some fashion observers and even fanatics found themselves utterly jaded, feeling they'd absolutely overdosed on clothes. But on a closer analysis, they'd overdosed on something very specific: menswear looks. Come fall, New York streets may well look either like a British gentlemen's club or like an outpost of Radclyffe Halls and Gertrude Steins, as the city fills up with a vast panoply of tweed and camel's hair overcoats, classic sweaters, men's shirts, and tailored pants, worn with ties and a myriad of other boyish accessories. But, heaven knows, it's the name of the game: every season, fashion is expected to stand on its head and to provide something completely different. And one can be almost certain that the very fashion professionals whose enthusiasm is exhausted now, will, several months hence, be energetically anticipating something new from their front-row collections seats. And the only thing that could really startle now is a healthy measure of old-fashioned feminine allure: soft dresses, bows, ruffles and even ballgowns. After seeing Tina Chow make a stunning entrance in a long, bustle-effect Empress Eugenie gown at a Karl Lagerfeld gala in New York, I'm hoping for a revival of tight lacing, beauty marks, fainting spells, and even the seductive language of fans.

One reason American designers were so resolutely clean and sportive this spring and fall is that design here is usually predicated on a certain realism – and in New York reality tells us that work for most women is a highly important part of their lives. While American women want to look good, they hope to do it without nonsense and furbelows, and they want safe clothes in which they can feel secure, correct, and powerful . . . clothes they can go to their jobs in and take nice healthy walks in the country. But after the past two seasons, it feels as if there's been a little too much sanity and not enough nonsense. It's time to bring back champagne tastes, and a bit of glamor and wit, flirtation, and even a little harmless deviousness. After all, in the words of hard-working singer Cyndi Lauper, "Girls just want to have fun".

THE JAPAN COLLECTIONS

Harris Gaffin

● "Fashion designers are the rock stars of the Eighties," architect Kiyohiko Umagami said sipping champagne. The occasion was the opening of the Yin & Yang boutique and office building in Daikonyama, a highly fashionable and expensive area of Tokyo. This is the place to be seen when president and designer, Katsushige Muraoka, pulls up at the entrance door driving his white BMW 733. The future of Japanese fashion has swerved through some hairpin turns this year and several fashion organizations have crashed.

The Tokyo Collection, which had intentions of sending out show tickets with just one call, the Japan Fashion Fair, set up to coordinate the efforts of apparel manufacturers, and the Best Five, a festive black-tie affair presenting the world's fashion superstars, all closed their offices.

To find the old Tokyo collection designers these days, you have to look to Paricorre (Japanese/English for Paris Collection). The nucleus of Japanese designers who are seeking a world-wide audience has expanded but the substantial increase in Japanese designers doing Paris, and perhaps later New York, is not the result of any organizational efforts by Japanese fashion makers.

It is part of the universal game called "keeping up with the Tanakas". If your competitor shows in Paris, you do too. The showing for many designers is to impress Japanese consumers of the designer's internationality. It can also be explained as very important for staff morale and naturally has nothing to do with a designer just wanting to say they showed in Paris!

In Japan, fashion sales have been steadily declining as the babyboom moves closer to mortgage payments but you wouldn't know it walking around the fashionable parts of Tokyo (Daikonyama included).

In Omote-Sando, Issey Miyake opened two new boutiques; Issey Miyake Men and Plantation. Plantation this year features rich shades of

HARRIS GAFFIN

● KANSAI YAMAMOTO

warm brown and is selling as fast as it can come into the store.

Issey has reason to celebrate and maybe that's why he often has parties, inviting jet-setters and journalists.

One such event was a Tokyo version of the Issey Miyake Pariscorre. Half-a-dozen full-length body casts were made of each of his top models. The plaster casts were then draped in fashions from the spring collection and placed in groups of motionless mannequins. There were half-a-dozen Hidekas and Takemis.

When the music started to play, the original models, who had been standing motionless in the exact same position as their mannequins, emerged from their group towards the audience and softly displayed the fashion in an original choreographed folk dance. The audience loved it.

Pashu, designed by Shin Hosakawa, moved to a new building in Roppongi and this year showed their first women's collection. The boutique is very graphic with abstract metal sculptures at the front and rear of the floor space. The walls are unpolished metal, dark earthy colors, the welding marks and natural pipes are part of the high tech environment.

The women's collection, like the men's, is also very new wave, featuring exaggerated high collars and large buttons and pocket flaps. Jacket cuffs and pants pockets featured flaps and buttons. Mannequins at the show wore original cubist style masks and the lighting was harsh. Very Pashu.

At this year's Nicole show (there were four collections), models wore hats, not masks. There were flap hats from the Twenties to go with long knit silhouettes. There were Scottish berets to match kilt-like skirts (also worn by men very effectively in the Monsieur Nicole collection). Camping hats were coordinated with knickers. Turban style hats coordinated with white gloves and jackets reminiscent of British colonial days. Pants were high waisted, collars clean, one pieces featured stripes at the waist. The collection made women look attractive. And, oh yes, there was a party celebrating the remodeling of the Nicole office and boutique in Gaenmae (half-way between Roppongi and Omote-Sando).

Hiroko Koshino is based in Osaka, four hours by Bullet train from Tokyo, so the Tokyo fashion show set doesn't see much of her during the year.

Down in Osaka people have their own language and own ideas. This year Hiroko Koshino continued to experiment with "chemical" (synthetic) yarn, adding geometric shapes to her hand knit collection. "Our job is to develop new yarn," she says energetically. That includes a hollow "macaroni yarn". The use of synthetic yarn gives her options unavailable with natural wool. "Guruguru" (wrap around) fabric would be oppressively heavy with the volume she has designed. With the macaroni yarn it is light and playful. Other imitation fabrics are possible like "fa" (fur) yarn, racoon, suede and arupaku.

Ideas come from the farm as well as the lab, such as featured patches of checkers inspired by the traditional

● JUNKO KOSHINO

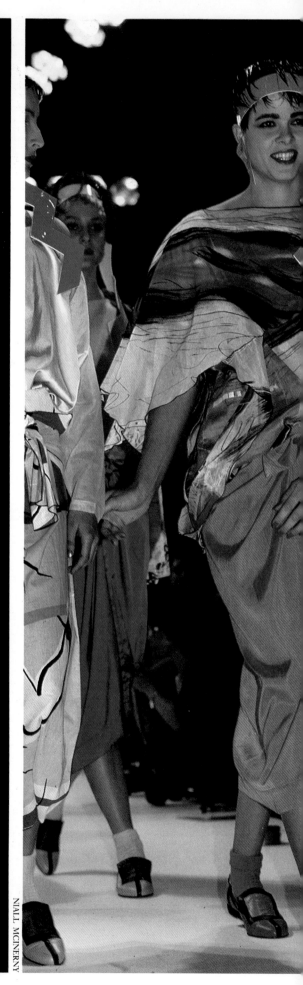

farmer's baskets used to carry vegetables in the Akita prefecture.

Jergen Lehl is one of the few foreign designers in Japan. He designs his own fabric and works freely, adding his own interpretations to basic themes. This year he mixed color based on his travels throughout Asia. He ordered fabric at the same width as kimono fabric (approximately 15 inches). All the fabric is shown, none is cut. Colors are similar to Korean celadon (pottery), light pastels of pinks and greens. The fabric is randomly striped cotton and very thick. The edge is fringed and used as it is. A skirt for example, is made from three pieces. Lehl works in a warehouse by the harbor. Zoning laws won't allow Hammamacho to become another SoHo, but everybody would like the sort of potential loft space which Jurgen has.

This year Studio V moved its offices into the building next door to Jurgens. With all this space, designer Erie still prefers to work out of his Paris office.

The nearby Jun Company, with more than 30 fashion lines, took warehouse space, set up a fashion radio station and broadcast a fashion television report, beaming into all Jun boutiques.

Adding to the Jun family is a new line called George Sand, designed by Kuniko Ikeda. Kuniko had an eye on the kimono market. Japanese schoolgirls traditionally wear kimonos at their graduation ceremony so Ikeda, with typical Jun entrepreneurship, designed a short jacket, coordinated it with a grey tuxedo shirt, and a black polka dot matching bowtie and waistband. The jacket is available in a black and white checkered pattern to compete with the kimono. The bottom, originally a mini-skirt, was expected to be the best seller but, surprisingly, black, slim ski-pants have been outselling the mini-skirt.

"I wish I had the money to dress up," says designer Atsuro Tayama, wearing a pair of jeans and a gray sweatshirt. He is president of a hot new label called AT (his initials). "Whatever I make, I've got to reinvest

● PINK HOUSE

● KANSAI YAMAMOTO

● OBSCURE DESIRE OF THE BOURGEOISIE

HARRIS GAFFIN

back into the company." Less status conscious, more themselves, Atsuro Tayama is part of a better traveled group of young professionals who speak for themselves, not for their company.

Tayama, like many of Japan's established designers, graduated from the Bunka Fukuso Gakkuen. He worked with Yohji Yamamoto in Paris and has seen enough of the world to have his job and responsibilities in perspective. "I have my own ideas of what I would like to do," says IS (part of the Issey Miyake group) designer Chisato Mori. "But my main priority is to satisfy the company's needs. After that I can experiment."

Mori and Tayama were classmates at Bunka. As for her own feelings towards fashion, "I'm a woman," she says, "and I want to design things that I intend to wear for myself."

This year's collection of "sporty casuals" is the IS bread and butter. Clothes are functional and comfortable to move around in. A fabric tie belt, cap, kit bag accessories. Tights under an apron-like dress, loose and comfortable. IS inaugurated the line with its first fashion show this year.

An alike minded individual, graduating the same year as Tsujimori and Tayama, is Hiroko Yamauchi of Accoustage. "I want to design cosmopolitan clothes for women; evening wear," she starts seriously, then smirks with frustration at the situation. "But the market is all about youngsters, they don't want serious adult clothes." "Kanko", as her friends call her, gained valuable experience in Paris. She is kept busy in her Daikonyama boutique and does not get to see her classmates much these days.

This year Hiroko Kido is taking on the "adult" challenge and launching her lingerie line "Tatoo". "We are aiming for the upper middle class woman. It is not a big market," she adds. "In America and Europe, adults have a master bedroom. Sexy lingerie has a chance to be seen. In Japan, only the well-off can afford spacious bedrooms." Tatoo is inspired from the "juban", usually worn as an

● ISSEY MIYAKE

HARRIS GAFFIN

YOHJI YAMAMOTO

JUNKO SHIMADA

HIROKO KOSHINO

undergarment to the kimono and its shape is similar to that of a chemise. Geisha girls wear it in vivid colors to attract customers. "It is a little decadent" Hiroko adds with a smile, "but it is sensual, not erotic."

From the classical juban shape, Hiroko added a slit up the side, making it easier to move. Where the back usually has an akamon (an emblem of the family symbol) stitched on the back, now a lace rose neatly replaces it. The most important adaptation is French lace sewn on the sleeves and collar, tracing down to the hem, replacing the customary Japanese print. The lace and silk combinations include gray and purple, purple and mustard, peach and beige and red and white.

"This oriental influence is intended for westerners, and once the Americans wear it, the Japanese will hopefully copy that lifestyle," Hiroko laughs, "and then maybe I can sell here without any problems."

Bright colors have always been a part of Japanese fashion tradition but that is where its relationship with Hitomi Okawa, Obscure Desire of the Bourgeoisie designers (often referred to as ODOB) ends.

Featured in this year's show were items such as three inch platform basketball sneakers, footlong baseball hats and seemless rubber one-piece dresses. "Wearing ODOB is like going to a costume party," says 22-year-old fashion expert Makiko Kunimatsu. Hitomi did not get much coverage in the foreign press. Maybe that is because any journalist who did not arrive at least an hour early, simply could not get to a seat. Her shows are packed beyond capacity.

Hitomi is down to earth and friendly. At her last show, instead of nervously preparing back stage, she was in front taking tickets and escorting guests personally to their seats.

Kansai. Well, Kansai is Kansai: bright colors and lots of tee shirts and sweat shirts taken from characters out of Japanese folklore. He continues to enjoy a clique following in major fashion capitals. Lots of writing on

● Combination of Japanese juban and French lace, photographed in an Akasaka Geisha House "TATOO" BY HIROKO KIDO

55

shirts and lots of zippers. Kansai is an institution. He is the fifth point on the star of Japanese fashion. He should not be judged by the standards of hemlines, stitching, collars, tucks or pleats.

Pink House is a quiet self-contained organization, not prone to publicity and does not seem particularly anxious to export. On the back of their basketball jackets reads, "Club Pink House, Leave Me Alone." Pink House takes its inspiration from western folklore. Designs from Sweden, Finland, Scotland, even Lapland made an appearance in this year's show but all tailored to Pink House's distinctive style. Tops tucked into or hanging loose over large white billowy dresses. You may catch the ends of a petticoat peeping discreetly out or a shawl wrapped around the shoulders: the end result is always lovely femininity.

"Some designers want an all-Japan image and like to give the impression their ideas come from Japanese history or folk tradition," says Ms Ishikawa, press attaché for Yohji Yamamoto. "Sometimes we think Yohji is stereotyped as getting all his ideas from Japan."

Anyone attending a Yohji Yamamoto fashion show is not likely to leave thinking his ideas are the exclusive copyright of Japanese background. A beautiful macramé sweater with intricate patterns and design. The audience gasped. The material? Shoestring! The purpose was to emphasize texture. A dramatic silhouette shape with sleeves so long they touched the ground. The message? Volume and mass. "Some people always assume he is so serious," Ishikawa shakes her head in amazement. "They cannot imagine Yohji being satirical."

Yamamoto sometimes does refer to Japanese tradition. A "hogussi" pattern of the country kimono inspired several loose fitting designs. "This year he has really loosened up. I do not think it is possible to say there is a particular theme. His inspirations can come from anything that catches his fancy."

● PASHU

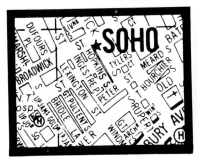

LONDON STREETS AHEAD

Iain R Webb

● It's hard to imagine any place where different cultures and colours live in harmony. It's an idyllic notion, but a place which *does* exist nevertheless. The streets of London have achieved a certain notoriety for the brightest, raciest, fastest-moving fashions. Colours, cultures and cuts which co-exist side by side.

Television researchers, in-tune reporters and sundry foreign correspondents line the pavements, vying for the best pictures, their cameras full of film and their pockets full of fifty pence pieces for their more astute victims. Even respected Fashion Editors nod in the direction of "The Street" when commenting on current designer looks. The turnover is fast, the attention-seeking furious. As soon as a "look" is worn by more than a handful, it is dropped by its original purveyors, only to be replaced by something equally loud and cocky.

The strength of these street fashions is their simplicity, their originality, and the adaptability of the wearer. One day you can dress in rags, the next in rich fabrics, dripping with jewellery. There are no restrictions, except those inside your own head.

Even society's established dress and sexual codes have recently been flouted, mocked, and often discarded altogether by today's trendier lifestylers ... and over the past year the newspapers have been feverish in their pursuit of Boy George or Marilyn or whoever follows in their satin slipstream.

There have been no rules in the street since Punk rejected and destroyed and left a legacy of new values. Values which include pride, strength and wild country wisdom – street sense: survival of the fittest and all that stuff.

The streets of London – and the streets of every major city – are inhabited by tribes, divided in appearance yet united by a common desire to be noticed, to survive, and to have a good time in the process.

But one fact is obvious. As soon as a fashion fad is adopted there will be a reaction against it. If the fashionable way to wear your hair is short, the trendies will wear it long ... eventually. The year 1983–4 was full of black and grey and depression chic until *someone* saw fit to wear a fluorescent flash of colour, and the world went day-glo... But within weeks of High Street overkill the trendies were pooh-poohing the whole look and dropping the colour fast. Trendsetters and Trendkillers. First in, first out.

The street is no longer a catwalk, as one earnest young reporter stated in the late Seventies. It has become *theatre*, and we all have the chance to take a starring role ... if we are bold enough, and bright enough, to do so!

● Right, *perhaps a reflection of the society we live in? Bruises (on both sexes) became fashionable, causing the more squeamish to wonder just what the world was coming to. Photo by Sally Boon.*

● *Diamonds used to be a girl's domain . . . until men like designer Gregory Davis grew their hair and plundered their mothers' jewellery boxes . . . sexual equality? Photo by Sally Boon.*

● Left, *for characters with cartoon appeal it was hip as long as it didn't fit. Too long, too short, too big, too small. Comic cuts. Photo by Iain McKell.*

● Inset, *shades of Sandra Dee. All a girl needs is a sweater . . . and the body and personality to fill it. Photo by Nick Knight.*

The Fleet was definitely IN! The more aesthetically-minded managed to sit through the movie Querelle; others simply donned sailors' caps and danced along to one-hit wonders, Roman Holliday. Clothes by BodyMap. Photos by Mike Owen.

● Above, *boys began to appear in discotheques dressed more appropriately for an athletics meeting than a night Uptown. Another racy fad was launched. Photo by Nick Knight.*

● Right, *in Chinatown, rough and heavy unstructured workwear was designed specifically to play in. Photo by Adrian Peacock.*

● Far right, *Bag Lady or Rag Lady, call it what you will — some found the look too close for comfort. But in New York crowds stormed Bloomingdales department store where such clothes were being sold at designer prices. These are by Rachel Auburn. Photos by Nick Knight.*

● Facing, *self-assured of their own sexuality, young ladies have become increasingly assertive and determined to make their presence felt in a (supposed) man's world . . . Photo by Nick Knight.*

● *A low, lean, V-backed dress was first sighted at Ronnie Scott's jazz club in Soho, worn by seductive songstress Sade Adu. It was last seen in every nightclub, on the back of every aspiring siren. Photo of Sade by Graham Smith.*

● *The group Jo Boxers just got lucky when they hit upon their Bowery image. Half-mast trousers, flat caps askew, braces and boots brought them even more hits. Photo by Mike Owen.*

STREET FASHION NYC

Karen Moline

Let's face it: Americans are lazy slobs at heart. Seventh Avenue propaganda notwithstanding, most New Yorkers take to the streets wearing conservative business suits for work and jeans or polyester for play. Perhaps it's latent Puritanical genes, but they are amazingly inhibited when it comes to outdoor displays of taste.

Those with a practised eye, however, can find fashion on the streets. It isn't hard. Anyone looking hip amid a sea of denim usually stands out. The best-put-together people usually look like they have just staggered out of an after-hours club at ten am. They probably have.

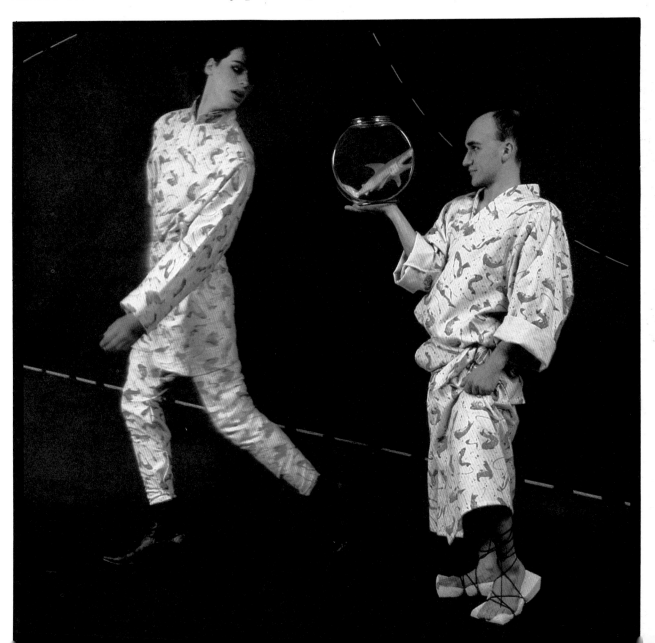

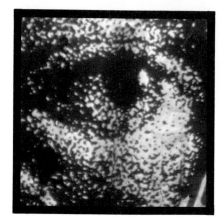

● Previous page, *pajamas are it for '84. Cotton flannel Louis XVI robe and pants by 22. Inspired by the street clothes of Cairo, designer Kelle Lebwith states: "Style is not a punctuated sentence." Photo by Kirk Winslow.*

● Above and below, *silkscreened Big Brother. Photo by Dana Fraser.*

● Right, *winter silhouette. Big coat and East Village attitude. Photo by Karen Moline.*

Truly Cool	*Fashion Victim*
One-of-a-kind garments from downtown design collectives or thrift stores	Anything from Bloomingdale's
Oversize jumpsuits from army surplus	Oversize jumpsuits from any store in SoHo
Levi's	Designer jeans
Hip-hop inspiration	Designer warmup suits
African or real tribal prints	Dayglo
Men's underwear as tee shirts	Keith Haring teeshirts
Pajamas and boxer shorts	Pants suits
Fur trim on clothes	Fur coats
Glacier glasses from a sporting goods store	Mirrored shades and a smirk

How To Make A Fashion Statement In The Streets

1. Wear anything remotely unconventional.

2. Do not respond to taunts and rude comments. Facial expression is all-important. In front of a mirror, practice the same affected pout featured in European fashion magazines. Never smile.

3. Do not appear self-conscious. That will ruin even the hippest outfit. Nor is gawking at other fashion victims acceptable – it's a dead giveaway that you're from New Jersey.

Now that you know what (not) to wear, apply this knowledge to the three categories of street dress you will find in NYC:

1. *All-American*
2. *East Village*
3. *SoHo*

● Right, *Beatnik revisited: beret, boatneck sailor sweater, black chinos, white socks and penny loafers. Photo by Karen Moline.*

● Far right, *singer Lauren Agnelli sports an Easter beret, leather bomber, pedal pushers and Sixties lace-up ghillies. Photo by Karen Moline.*

All-American

Your basic NYC slobbola will sport the following: jeans, athletic shoes, tee shirt or button-down oxford shirt, and a leather jacket if it's cold. Only permitted accessory: Sony Walkman. The semifashionable will move up a notch with cropped jeans, gladiator sandals, an off-the-shoulder *Flashdance* tee, and some brightly colored jewelry.

Most suppliers to the collegiate/preppie brigade are clustered on Broadway between 8th St. and Houston in the area known as NoHo. The two biggest stores are Unique and Canal Jeans, and even the truly hip can find trendy accessories (even as they state that as soon as anything makes an appearance in these mass-produced emporiums it's an automatic certification of passé). The goods are cheap, cool, and disposable after a season. What else d'ya want for the streets?

A browser will find Katharine Hamnett ripoffs, baggy Jap looks, dayglo socks, studded biker jewelry, pseudoAfrican prints, mesh tanks, overdyed tees, rayon Hawaiian shirts, army fatigues, pith safari hats, and all kinds of jeans and sweats for ridiculously low prices. A few snazzy items can enliven even a clone's wardrobe.

● Right, *the All-American. Artist Ronnie Cutrone in his uniform: US Olympic tee over striped tee from Agnes B, jacket from the Leather Man, Levi's and shoes from Playboy Clothing on 42nd Street. Photo by Karen Moline.*

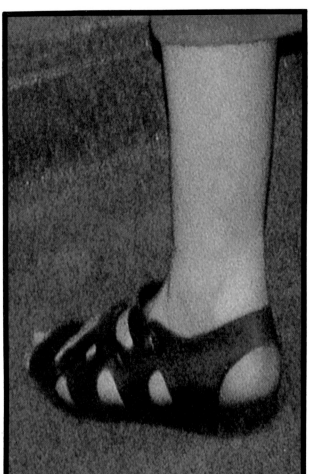

East Village

The evertrendy can hang out in the East Village to watch the parade of the postpunk generation that's younger, more adventurous, and far poorer than its SoHo counterpart. St. Mark's Place is the closest NYC has to King's Road, and the occasional starched and dyed hairdo will receive a proportionately shorter gawk and gasp than it would elsewhere. The basic EV style is eclectic and British-influenced (yes, people read *The Face* here), even though Spandex is still worn, and most poseurs look desperately anemic and in need of a week at the beach.

Preeminent purveyor for the Village is Patricia Field, which has been on 8th St. for ten years and carries a mix of NYC and British designers (much of her merchandise is available in shops on King's Road). You'll find everything from oversize white sportswear, huge droopy hand-knits, Williwear, sophisticated linen suits, rubber wetsuits, plaid boxer shorts, one-piece wrestling suits, and crayon-colored wigs to chunky space-age jewelry. The store presents a certain attitude: You have to have it to carry it off.

East a few blocks is the original punk store: Manic Panic, run by sisters Tish and Snooky, who buy much of their newer stock from people who come in from off the streets. Manic Panic is the only store to carry black lipstick and other necessary grooming aids for skinheads and terminal punkettes. An astute street watcher, Tish laments, "The same people who were laughing at us seven years ago are wearing those clothes now. Fashion gets so boring. People who have just one look don't realize they're getting into the same rut as their parents' polyester. Fashion is only fun if you can change."

Other stores of note: 109 St. Mark's, Einsteins, Modern Girls, Trash & Vaudeville, and Black Magic.

● Right, *mini '64 meets mini '84. Tish from Manic Panic wears a Sixties original suit; Venus, her fave model, wears an updated skirt and hand-knit sweater. The store sells anything from vintage spike heels to r'n'r tee shirts to tarty lingerie. Photo by Karen Moline.*

● Facing top, *one-of-a-kind hand knits in whimsical shapes inspired by kid's clothes and op-art patterns, worn with tight wool skirts and leggings. Designer Marc Jacobs says his clothes are "not about fashion, but about style". Photo by Julie Moline.*

● Facing below left, *the Real Thing. Street fashion takes off from breakers wearing casual athletic gear and baseball caps. Skaters tend to be bizarre. Photo by Karen Moline.*

● Facing below right, *attitude: "I just put things together on the slenderest of bases," says writer/ photographer Fred Goss. "People are like so many sheep. I'm totally alienated from any kind of corporate fashion – I like to startle." Jacket from a used clothes store; pants by Reminiscence; hand-painted shirt by Danilo.*

SoHo

In SoHo even upscale people can wear what they want. The most European of NYC's downtown neighborhoods, SoHo is chockfull of art galleries and exclusive boutiques featuring the best of Euro and American designers – Comme des Garçons, Suzanne Bartsch, Tous les Caleçons, Koos, Dianne B, Agnès B, Kenzo, Beged-Or, Betsey Johnson, and many more – at inflated prices (which precludes most street watchers from even browsing). SoHo fashion philosophy is perfectly expressed by Terry Hyland of Chaserie on West Broadway: "The basics don't sell at all. Women want something different, but not *too* much – they don't know what to do with it. Most customers need a whole lot of help."

On weekends, SoHo becomes a veritable feast for the senses. The teeming masses from suburbia descend to buy an outfit and accessories in which they can return the following weekend in an attempt to be trendy. At least they're trying.

The most interesting clothes on SoHo's streets are sported by gallery groupies on their way to openings, and these wearers actually have mastered the art of attitude. You'll see Japanese silhouettes, turbans, fantastic jewelry from Artwear, big black linen dresses cinched by hip-slung thick leather belts, nautical hats, layers of raggedy cottons and mesh in boxy cropped shapes, leather-trimmed yoked jeans by Guess?, huge geometric shapes from Parachute, and every kind of boxer shorts. And blunt-cut hair.

If only Americans would lose their inhibitions and flaunt their stuff. Fashion is entertainment, and people in NYC love to be entertained. What better way than to dress like your mood? In this city you have every occasion to live out your fantasies. Just take them to the streets.

● Top left, *the shape of coats to come. Miro-inspired print on wool. Designed by Robert Molnar. Model: Matthew Reed. Photo by David Kong.*

● Top right, *SoHo for men. Dan Robertas designed his leather skullcap. Top by Matsuda, pants by Marithe. Photo by Karen Moline.*

● Below left, *SoHo chic. Terry Hyland of Chaserie in cotton/linen overalls and vest by Risma, with diagonally slung chunky ceramic necklace. Photo by Karen Moline.*

● Below right, *summer silhouettes: African prints and figure-hugging solids. From Modern Girls. Photo by Tom Fraser.*

INTERVIEW: FASHION EDITOR SALLY BRAMPTON

Maxim Jakubowski • Emily White

● Sally Brampton studied at the fashion department of St Martin's School of Art where she discovered that her talents lay in fashion journalism rather than design. A special mention in the *Vogue* Talent Contest led to her working there for two years as a writer. At twenty-eight and Fashion Editor of *The Observer* she is one of a new breed of young fashion journalists.

You are the Fashion Editor of The Observer, *an influential post in the British press. How do you see your job, what does a fashion editor do and what are you trying to convey to your readers about the world of fashion?*

My work falls into two areas, it is an information service to the readers and attempts at the same time to describe fashion from a sociological point of view: how it's changing, how it's affecting people, how people's social lives are affecting it. It is a very good mirror of what is going on in society. I try to balance my pages between, say, summer frocks and some item of interest, like the effect of ragged denim and the "Hard Times" look that was going on in the street, or men growing their hair, men wearing jewellery, covering matters from a lot of different angles.

I think it's terribly dull to say "Here are three summer frocks, these are three spring suits" every week. I don't know if you've ever tried to write 800 words on three spring suits but it's not easy. What we do for our readers is to shop on a mass scale. We shop for about half a million women. We research the market and pull out what we feel is the best, in both price and quality. I attempt to keep my prices down unless I feel that it is justified by a designer whose clothes are so influential that you can't get them elsewhere and who is obviously going to have an impact on the mass market.

What many people have against fashion pages in newspapers and magazines is that a lot of the outfits chosen are in fact beyond

the reach of the average reader.

Well, that's what people say, but if you actually sit down and analyse my pages, say over the past year, they are not. I tend to be a socialist about fashion, in the sense that I don't believe in high-pricing. This is why we attempt to cover everything from Marks & Spencer, through Next to Alexon. I wouldn't use cheap clothes if I didn't feel that the quality was up to it. And as I maintain, I would use designer clothes if I thought there was a reason for doing so.

How did you become a fashion editor?

When I left school I had a place at university to read history. But I took

a year off and worked as a waitress and my whole conception of the world changed from living on my own and supporting myself. I suddenly realised that I wasn't cut out to be an academic, that what I really wanted to do was fashion. I took some more time off and worked as a waitress for another year and then I applied to St Martin's and got in.

I was a very mediocre designer; in my second year they started the journalism course. I began to write and realised that I was much better writing about fashion than I was at actually designing it.

In our third year we were supposed to have a placement in industry for a minimum of three months to qualify for our degree. It was at that time when the recession was striking very badly. Jobs in fashion journalism were few and far between, so I did the *Vogue* Talent Contest and was one of the runners up. I was a special mention, I didn't win it. I was then very fortunate that there was a vacancy in the Fashion department at *Vogue*, they needed an assistant so I joined them. I spent two years training there which was, I think, just the best training in the world. I worked for Beatrix Miller who is one of the great editors. She was always incredibly encouraging. I'd bounce in saying I wanted to do this or that piece, I was about to change the world, about to change the face of British fashion. She'd say "go away and research it darling, and we'll have a look." I did odd bits and pieces and then I started to do copylines. Then the copywriter was ill so I was suddenly landed with writing copylines, headlines and coverlines. Liz Tilberis, my fashion editor, and I started between us to do the Cue pages, Liz was the editor and I was the writer on it, and then after about six months I was left to do it on my own. They became my pages and I continued to write everything else. I was sent to all the collections to do the internal and external reports for the magazine; then *The Observer* rang me up.

Many people feel that British fashion has been very much at the forefront over the last few years. Are you, as a British fashion writer, excited by what is happening?

Oh yes, I always have been terribly chauvinistic about my own country and I believe very strongly in our fashion ideas. I think that the problem with this country regarding fashion is that we are very unprofessional when it comes to promotion and the business side. If you just look at the way our shops present merchandise compared to Italy or America you can see the difference immediately. If you asked a store buyer in America, "What do you do?", you would get a ten minute lecture about how wonderful they were. Whereas if you asked Clare Stubbs who is one of the most powerful women in British retailing at Harvey Nichols she would say, "Oh I'm just a buyer", it's that sort of difference in attitude. I think we have a huge energy here although we suffered very badly in the Seventies, there was a sort of post-Sixties depression.

We've always had a very, very creative youth element in our streets.

Do you feel that this resurgence, of interest is echoed overseas? Does New York, for instance, have the same image of British fashion that we have here?

Well, we are the sort of *enfant terrible* of the fashion world. A lot of it is to do with the extreme looks we produce and what the kids are wearing on the street. They think we are wonderful and daring because we are so outrageous.

There was a period about two years ago when everyone was rushing around saying how terrific the new young British designers were and the buyers were wringing their hands at bad quality and poor deliveries but a whole new group is changing that and I think that the buyers and manufacturers in this country are working with them. Everybody is beginning to make a team that will promote British fashion, young British fashion. Designers like Jean Muir and Janice Wainwright have been around for a long time, they're wonderful and their clothes are terrific but they don't really spearhead anything new. This is a whole new movement in fashion.

Do you feel there is any competition between fashion editors, insofar as you can encourage or promote one particular

It hasn't always been reflected in the mass market or our designer names. But that's changing, I think it has a lot to do with our manufacturers who are using designers more. The public are also becoming more aware of fashion, more aware that they can buy good quality, well designed clothes at moderate prices. The whole system is changing here, and I'm very pleased that it's happening.

NATHALIE LAMORAL.

EVA SERENY   EVA SERENY   EVA SERENY

designer or another, or is there more of a general feeling of solidarity in promoting fashion as a whole?

There is a great feeling of solidarity, in fact we amaze our overseas colleagues, they think we are quite extraordinary. They think we are terribly sweet because we rush off to collections and we are not open to bribery and corruption in the same sense that they are. As a whole, all fashion editors get on very well. Of course, if you are a journalist you want an exclusive, you don't necessarily fight for that exclusive but if you happen to know one designer better than another then you're more likely to get that exclusive, but I think that's as far as it actually goes.

Early on in my career, I was contacted by the PR who was responsible for Next. I got the first story and went up to the factory to interview George Davis, the MD. So you can regard that as an exclusive because Next was big news. The PR in that case was extremely clever and extremely honest. She said she was placing it with a Daily and with a Sunday. So I was the Sunday and the Daily was *The Daily Mail*. This was a very wise move because our readership doesn't really clash, whereas if somebody placed it with *The Guardian* and with *The Observer* it would have been that much more difficult because we tend to clash on readership.

Are there designers that you take a particular interest in? Can you really have an effect on the career of a designer?

To a certain extent you can give them

publicity and make them a known name but it's up to them to follow that up by producing the quality and the orders. One must be objective, I don't think that you should back any single designer. I take an interest in the young designers as a group because I find them exciting at the moment, which is not to say that I neglect any of the other designers or the general mass market.

Do you have regular contacts with buyers or are you just an "observer" on the scene?

Fairly regular. I try and keep in contact as much as possible with them. For instance, if I was doing a story on coats, I'd want to speak to the outerwear buyers at the major stores about how sales were going, what was selling best, because that's really where we get our information from. It's all very well to be a fashion journalist stuck in an office somewhere but if you just don't actually know what is moving, what is selling, what the public want, then it's more difficult.

How do you spend your working week?

I spend five days a week on *The Observer* from ten to seven every day. As well as doing the newspaper, I do the magazine and at the moment we seem to be turning out a magazine story about once a week as well as a newspaper column.

What people don't understand about fashion journalists is that they research the market which takes a lot of time then they have to set up and attend all their photo sessions. They study everything with real interest and

● *Sportswear turned inside-out. Styled by Sally Brampton. Photos by Wayne Stambler for The Observer.*

do all the styling which means everything from accessories to make-up. They have to book the hairdressers, models, make-up artists, studio and check the location as well as organising the actual story, interviewing people and doing the research.

Also you tend to be an ambassador for your own newspaper in the sense that you will probably be involved in a number of business lunches and business drinks, just for the sake of maintaining a high profile for your newspaper or for your pages. We also have an awful lot of paper to push around, we get stacks of press releases, then we do all our special offers, merchandising and invoicing. We are expected to do most of the styling for other departments. Say they need a guy to wear a suit, we have to get that suit in for them. It's a very physical job because we've got clothes coming in and clothes going out. They all have to be booked in, they all have to be booked out, so it's a very intricate system. People tend to think that fashion journalists keep the clothes, but anything that goes missing has to be paid for. Nothing is actually kept, it all goes back.

The magazine tends to be more orientated towards styling. There are two forms of fashion editors, there is a fashion stylist, and a fashion journalist and in a magazine you are more likely to find yourself a stylist than you are a journalist although it is in journalism that my interests lie.

Is it important for a fashion editor to have a rapport with a photographer whom they can use regularly?

Well, I use Nathalie Lamoral a lot for collections work. The collections are so frantic and those photographers go through such hell, plus they have their editors screaming at them because they've missed an essential picture, I work with Nathalie because she's always cheerful.

During the collections we do a number of peripheral stories which you will see reflected in the magazine and in the newspaper throughout the next six months. This is really a way of justifying your budget because it's very expensive to go away. Nathalie's wonderful because she will never throw a wobbly, she'll never say no. She's lugging huge great camera cases around, dragging them through the rain when I need a portrait done somewhere and she's very versatile. She's also very experienced at catwalks which is a completely different art to, say, news photography which is why I don't use somebody from *The Observer*. You have to know how to get into those shows and how to deal with them. There are so many photographers, you have to be able to get in there. She shoots on two cameras, it's very hard work.

When you organise a session for the magazine or the newspaper what sort of criteria do you have for choosing models?

I always choose someone who is going to suit the feature I am doing. We are in touch with all the major model agencies, and I work with the photographers on selection. For example, we are shooting six black and white photographs this afternoon,

● *Japanese designers have been heralded as the most exciting new movement in fashion since the Sixties. Rough weaves and loose layers mark a departure from European tradition. Styled by Sally Brampton. Photos by Nathalie Lamoral.*

three of them are the feature for next Sunday, the story is designers who do cheaper ranges under different names, and three pictures are for the "best buys" section in our newspaper. So the girl has got to fit into a combination of Betty Jackson, Barbara de Vries and Benny Ong. Then she's got to be able to carry a little silk frock from C&A and also a nautical white blazer, so she's got to be versatile.

A lot of our week is spent having models coming and going and I take a lot of time with photographers, hairdressers and make-up artists who want to come and show us their books and students who might need help or advice. When we're shooting we try and save money by shooting more than one story in a session. We can't have two stories running on consecutive Sundays with the same model in them so we have to have a bank of stories that we can build up and interchange.

You mentioned earlier that there are a lot of incentives and there is possible corruption. Can you mention some examples of people trying to influence you for commercial gain?

It does not really happen so much in this country. There was one occasion when somebody said that if I wrote a piece I could have an outfit. I didn't want the outfit, I wouldn't have worn it if it was given to me free, apart from anything else. But a lot of that does go on in Europe, money changes hands, that kind of number. The fashion editors in Europe expect not to pay for their clothes because, from the designer's point of view, they are their personal PR and if someone is wearing their clothes they are giving them their stamp of endorsement.

Do you feel a fashion editor can "burn out" after a certain time?

It depends on the individual. Some are immortal, they can go on and on and on. It depends on the nature of your readership as well. If you feel as a fashion editor that you should be in touch with everything; from street level, to the manufacturers, to high design, it's a very exhausting task,

because you have to go to the clubs, you have to travel, you have to go down the King's Road, you have to see what is happening in the music industry, which directly affects fashion.

From my own point of view I think that one can become very weary of fashion. I'm very lucky that my newspaper allows me to develop a real story as opposed to caption write pictures. So in that sense I don't get bored with what I do. They also allow me a certain variety. But I think that if I had to trot out captions, week after week after week, it would drive me completely bananas.

I also tend to be more interested in the peripheries that surround fashion than in the three little frocks, and it doesn't interest me to dictate to my readers what they should wear. I think that my function as a fashion editor is to show what is available, what's around and what is newsworthy. Then they have the choice as to whether they go out and buy something. I think to say you must wear *that* this summer but you mustn't wear *this* is frightfully out of date. We have a catholic choice now in fashion in the shops anyway. I know there are certain looks, there are certain pervading atmospheres that coin a pattern and you can fall within that but still have an awful lot of variety.

Do you find it interesting that the styles of people in the music business in the UK are beginning to affect fashion?

I think they always have. The obvious parallel is the Sixties and I think the same thing is happening again. In addition we have young designers like Dexter Wong or BodyMap designing for people like Boy George, Frankie Goes to Hollywood, or the Thompson Twins. There are no fashion programmes on television, the only way some kids see fashion is on their favourite groups and their clothes become famous through the fact that what they wear gets wanted.

Do you have any particular feelings about what is happening in America, or the directions in which American fashion is progressing?

As fashion moves in cycles, so fashion countries move in cycles and I think New York has been through its heyday and is on the decline in terms of interest, of excitement generated amongst the press, the buyers, the readers.

I think that our experience of New York has been incredibly valuable because they've taught us about real commercialism, real professionalism, real promotion, real presentation. The manufacturers are mass market manufacturers, they talk in millions there, here we talk in hundreds, they are very clever and they provide a certain sort of style.

I think the only two real designers working in New York are Perry Ellis and Norma Kamali, she's a genius. But then again I would probably only name two who are brilliant in Italy or Paris, the rest of them are very clever promotional people, very clever because they diversify into other products and build up multi-million empires.

As a fashion editor/writer could you function in New York if you went to work on an American publication?

No, because I hate the style of journalism there, journalese like "kicky skirts and flirty hemlines". I can't bear it. It's more superficial, but it's much more serious. The Americans are incredibly professional as journalists, but they tend to lack humour and I find that American fashion lacks humour, the Americans lack humour in the way they dress. I don't think I could work in New York, it would drive me completely insane.

Where do you see your future?

Where? At the moment I suppose I'm really moving towards the area of features more than anything else. I'd like to write books and my ultimate ambition is to edit a magazine which will probably happen to me when I'm in my forties, that's what I'd like to do but I don't know whether it will happen, we all move off at such tangents. I was going to be an historical researcher ten years ago. I don't know what I'll be doing in another ten years.

NATHALIE CAVENDISH
STYLIST

● **The job title "Stylist" is so ambiguous that it can cover any number of visual fields. It is a blanket term for someone who performs a service to a creative media industry that may have the ideas but not the time, inclination or contacts to realise them. Essentially, a stylist is there to listen to other people's ideas and put them into practice. An adequate stylist will live up to the brief. A really good one will inject style and life into it.**

A stylist may be called upon by the art director of an advertising agency, who will first produce a series of layouts or story boards. A story board is basically a series of very simple cartoons or line drawings which indicate to the stylist the atmosphere, period, social class and colour scheme of the furniture and clothes that they wish him or her to provide in order to bring that concept to life.

Within the field of styling there are many specialised areas. These are likely to evolve as the stylist's instincts, contacts, experience and confidence increase. A stylist who specialises in room sets is unlikely to be asked to style a fashion shoot, but a fashion journalist or editor, already an expert in the field, would be an ideal choice. A specialist food stylist would not necessarily be a home economist, but might well work closely with one, finding the right utensils and backdrops to match the mood of the food.

Some stylists will concentrate on studying locations intensively, amassing immense catalogues of unusual buildings and settings. If a 17th Century church in a quiet seaport is needed as a backdrop for a shoot, they will know of one, or know exactly where to find one.

One of the stylist's most important possessions is an address book. This will contain information about everything, from people to props, including PR agents, property suppliers and modelling agencies most likely to be able to provide exactly who is needed. These contacts are usually developed through working for other people: fashion editors, senior stylists, art directors, PR offices, photographers, studios and so on. Along with all her other contacts, a stylist will know good agencies specialising in all types of models and will be able to cast, knowing exactly who is appropriate, who is available and where to find them. But only experience can build up this pool of information since senior stylists tend to guard their contacts jealously.

A telephone is indispensable. Half a stylist's working day is spent on the phone, juggling with art directors, clients, models, set builders, model makers and photographers, all of whom will eventually, hopefully, agree about a particular brief. The rest of the day is usually spent in the car. After a morning on the telephone to all her contacts, a stylist will have a more precise idea of where to find these props, models and locations. Now the physical slog starts, she has to see exactly what and who is available before making a final choice and the car is a must, not only for transport, but also as a temporary home for all the essential bits and bobs until they get to the studio.

At the outset, a stylist is likely to have to take on fairly unglamorous work requiring a good deal of footwork. But like any other field, one has to work up the ladder in order to get more sophisticated assignments.

However, mere contacts and experience are not enough. Trust, taste, personality and instincts are all essential. A stylist will have to build up a relationship with her clients so that they learn to trust her instincts and taste. Many briefs are vague and she will be expected to be able to understand the general feel of the concept immediately in order to put it into action. And, at the end of the day, the nebulous nature of the stylist's work is only as part of a team who are in the business of selling. If the campaign is successful and the product sells, then she has fulfilled her brief, and justified her fee.

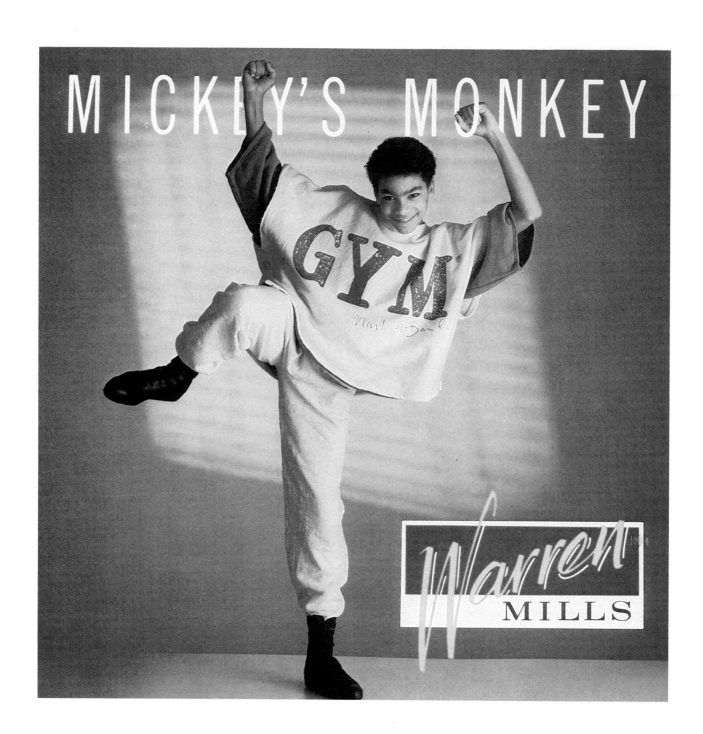

MICKEY'S MONKEY

Warren MILLS

Warren Mills record cover, Jive records, John Sims at Zomba, photographed by Eric Watson.

What does one do with a talented young 11-year-old lad and a small budget? One rents and borrows and doesn't buy. Throw a few outfits and suggestions into the studio and voilà.

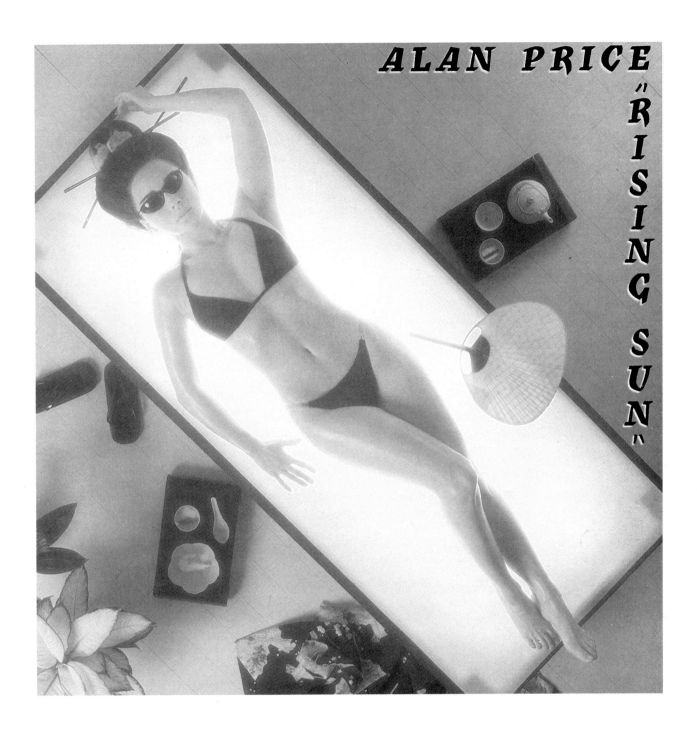

ALAN PRICE
"RISING SUN"

Alan Price record cover for Jet records. Photographed by Gered Mankowitz.

In this case a set had to be built. The bed the model is lying on had to be made to measure in the studio and the props are from an Oriental Arts dealer in London. The plastic food, crockery, fan and chop sticks are on loan from Liberty. The plants were bought and the model was the photographer's choice. Scaffolding had to be erected high above the set, for Gered to shoot from.

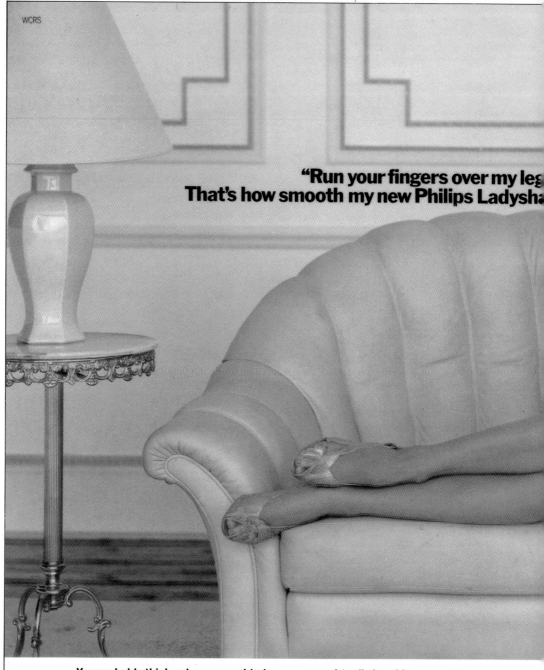

Philips Ladyshave – Photographed by Terence Donovan – Styled by Kari Allen. Wight Collins Rutherford Scott.
Kari was contacted by Terence Donovan's girl friday, Angela, for the styling of the Philips Ladyshave ad. She arranged to have a meeting with Ron Collins, Creative Director for Wight Collins Rutherford Scott; a very particular and high powered art director.

"I had worked with Donovan and Ron Collins before, so I was prepared for this to be a tough job." *She was shown a very specific layout, everything*

had to be creams and beiges so that nothing would detract from the model's silky, smooth legs.

"Donovan had organised the model casting already and had chosen Beska, so I tackled the props. Two small elegant tables, two lamps, a beige carpet and a sofa. The choice was up to me, within the confines of the brief. Considering there are many good prop houses in London, that wasn't too tricky."

But Kari had to scout around quite a bit for the sofa as it had to be in immacu-

late condition and, although the prop houses stock all kinds of furniture for stills, films and television, they are not always in the best state. This one is leather and just needed slight touching up with hide food.

She was given two days' preparation and it was to be a two day shoot. The background was a plain white wall and Donovan arranged for one of his expert set builders to mock up the beading the day before the shoot. Clothes and jewellery were next on the list.

"I went to several PR's who have

es them."

(Just think. No more tweaking or wincing from wax or razor nicks!)
You can feel the difference on your legs after a single shave.
Until then you can feel the difference on these.

PHILIPS

collections in their offices and will sometimes, after a certain amount of persuasion, hire clothes for advertising shoots, but no-one is keen unless there is to be a credit for the designer. There was nothing simple enough for our requirements, so I began to comb the shops and arranged to borrow several outfits from Browns on approval. I also nipped in to Jasper Conran's showroom and left with a couple of outfits. Altogther there were ten possibilities for Ron Collins to choose from, all expensive and fragile,

it was nerve racking carrying them around, knowing how much they cost."

The shoes were by Maud Frizon, hired from Browns, and the jewellery was from Butler & Wilson. Again Kari had to get about three times the amount actually needed for optimum choice.

"We had a test day, which for a stills shot like this is quite unusual. Everything was set up; model, make-up artist and hairdresser were all at the studio. We made the final selection of clothes etc, did the shot, then

the film was processed to check that all the details were correct."

They all came back the next day to do the real thing. While the hair and make-up was being done, Kari returned the clothes that were not selected for the final choice, to cut down the hiring expenses. The dress that was finally chosen, was a totally plain and simple silk satin shift by Jasper Conran.

"I'm sure the finished product looks effortless and indeed the shoot went very smoothly. No sleep was lost, but that is not always the case."

THE NE

Under the bonnet of the new
Corolla GT Coupé lurks a truly
awesome lump of power.

It's a rally bred 1587cc, 4-cylinder,
twin overhead cam, 16-valve engine
with electronic fuel injection.

And it's the main reason why
the GT Coupé out-performs every
other car in its class.

But there are other reasons.

With a Cd factor of 0.35,
it's aerodynamically better than

a Po

set
spe
get

PRICE AT TIME OF GOING TO PRESS: £6995.35 INCLUDES CAR TAX, VAT AND SEAT BELTS. EXCLUDES NUMBER PLATE

3BHP COROLLA GT COUPÉ.

arrera.
box is so expertly
unce of torque
t and you don't
s.
steering, plus anti-

roll bars front and rear, keeps everything on the straight and narrow
and totally under your control.
Especially as you have dual
circuit, servo-assisted brakes, with
ventilated discs up front, to cool

the pace down if it gets too hot.
The GT Coupé is a car that
generates 123.8bhp, does 0-60 in
8.3 seconds and has a top speed
of 122mph.
Which is a superb engineering

achievement. But not a surprising
one.
Because it's another thorough-
bred from the Corolla stable.
And the Toyota Corolla is the
car the world made perfect.

THE 16-VALVE, TWIN-CAM COROLLA GT COUPÉ.

TOYOTA

GES. TOYOTA (GB) LIMITED, HEAD OFFICE   AND PERSONAL EXPORT, THE QUADRANGLE, STATION ROAD, REDHILL, SURREY RH1 1PX. TELEPHONE: REDHILL (0737) 68585.

Chelsea Girl promotion co-ordinated by Lynne Franks PR. Styled by Debbi Mason, Photographed by Martin Brading

ST. MARTIN'S SCHOOL OF ART

Lydia Kemeny

● The top end of Charing Cross Road in London is noisy, dusty, and singularly unbeautiful. It is here that St Martin's School of Art sits sulkily behind its bland Thirties façade, shabby, cramped and inconvenient. The manually operated lifts, malevolent relics of a bygone technology, provide a daily challenge to all comers who would presume to use them to reach the upper floors.

Yet perhaps it is this tattiness and contrariness of the place that provokes the determination to get there, nourishes the creative spirit and produces the quintessential buzz that is St Martin's. It must certainly contribute to the element of wit that permeates much of what comes out of there, since only those with an unshakeable sense of humour can hope to flourish in such an environment.

There seems to be no record of the moment when St Martin's School of Art became just that. We believe that it is probably the oldest Art School in the UK and that it evolved from one

of the Art Academies known to have existed in the neighbourhood of the present school during the 18th Century. Rather a good century for the birth of a school destined to develop such a strong interest in Fashion that it would have the largest Fashion department in the country. However, at that time none of this could have been foreseen since fashion as we know it today did not exist.

Not until the 1930s did a few colleges begin classes in dress design: and then very much as the poor little relations of the Textiles courses that

flourished in the wake of the Arts and Crafts movement.

At St Martin's however, dress design was begun by Muriel Pemberton under the protective umbrella of the Graphics Department. While most dress design courses were largely concerned with dressmaking, she was interested in drawing, colour, texture and shape: the aesthetic aspects of dress. She believed Fashion at its best to be as much of an art form as textiles, ceramics or other design disciplines, and she instilled this belief into us, her students. This may not now seem

such a very strange concept, but until dress design was transformed into glamorous Fashion during the Sixties, it was as iconoclastic a belief as thinking the world to be round.

Teaching in art schools then was not at all structured and the dress design course ran very much along the same lines. Students congregated there because they had a passionate commitment to Art or Design and did not think too much about what they would do when they came out of college. Terms like "Marketing" or "Business Studies" had not entered the vocabulary and in any case it was not felt that these were areas that a designer could or should be concerned with. The clothing manufacturing industry in the UK saw no need for designers, it looked for pattern cutters who could, with any luck, knock off an idea seen in a magazine. Only a few brave employers would even contemplate giving a job to an art student with no experience.

The development of the Fashion Department at St Martin's is closely bound up with the development of the Fashion Industry itself. During the Fifties, fashion had begun slowly to acquire respectability and then suddenly, during the Sixties, it really took off. To be a fashion designer was almost as glamorous as being a pop star or a hairdresser. Sadly it often proved to be just as ephemeral, but while it lasted it was magic. Fashion became a means of self-expression, a living, exciting means of communication. There was an energy and an immediacy about it, it was accessible to almost everybody and for the first time there was audience participation. By the end of the decade, doing your own thing had begun to filter through to fashion in much the same way as it would eventually filter through to the whole colour supplement lifestyle of the Seventies. For the first time too, fashion was for the young.

For a young person interested in fashion, one of the most critical things to face is the need to assess whether it is worth their while pursuing that interest to career level or whether to be satisfied with buying or making something nice to wear.

There are easier ways of earning a living than working in fashion. However, true fashion addicts will not be deterred by such considerations, nor will they ultimately find it at all strange that, because a collection has to be finished, they are expected to work till late at night, start at the crack

of dawn for a photographic session, or stand in the Tuileries mud for six days, including the weekend, in order to see the Paris fashion shows. They will be so absorbed in the work that they will hardly notice.

Nearly all fashion careers will mean too little time to meet deadlines, endless crises over money, fabrics, buyers, models and fashion shows, an unevenly spread workload and fatigue. But there will also be the joy of doing a job you love, the fun of working with people who have similar interests, travel, and, of course, sometimes the ultimate reward of all creative ambitions: acclaim.

The British cherish a curious nostalgia for the obsolete practice of workroom apprenticeship but fashion today is so far removed from the dressmakers and the ladies' journals of the past that it seems patently obvious that fashion designers working with factories scattered across the world need very different skills to the ones that were required to impress a private clientele.

But if the apprenticeship system is to be regarded as obsolete what do the colleges teach? Can you teach creativity? The answer must be no, it is not possible to instil creativity where there is none. But a creative talent can be recognised and it can be guided to acquire the disciplines and skills necessary to its development and, possibly even more critically, its regeneration. This is an arduous process and intelligence, self-motivation and tenacity are needed as well as talent if a student's creative potential is to be fully realised.

The talents of fashion students do not all lie in the same direction and, at St Martin's, we encourage this diversity rather than trying to fit everyone into one mould. We try to develop the students' aesthetic perceptions and their sensitivity to what is going on, not just in fashion but in other spheres too, since fashion does not exist in isolation but is simply one means of expressing the spirit of the time. We stress the need for technical proficiency as this is essential to design thinking. You cannot give clear instructions to technical staff and factories if you do not know how the whole process works and have not thought it through. Another tenet is the absolute necessity of coming to terms with the commercial realities of finance, marketing and promotion. Bankrupt businesses do not employ designers.

● Previous page, *sweatshirts peel off to reveal "I-K-E" vests by Ike Rust. Photo by Graham Murrell.*

● Above, *Katharine Hamnett "Save The World Now".*

FEVER

KATHARINE HAMNETT
LONDON

KATHARINE

STOP
KILLING WHALES

KATHARINE
HAMNETT,
LA PROVOCATRICE
DELLA MODA

If all this sounds somewhat solemn it is because, in part, it has to be. Fashion today is a serious business but it is also meant to be fun. If a new outfit doesn't give you a lift then what is it for? In the more affluent societies of today, consumers do not buy clothes purely out of modesty or to keep warm. They buy largely to satisfy that inborn characteristic of the human race, the urge for something new – and new clothes are one of the easiest and most accessible ways to achieve this satisfaction. Just how different that "something new" has to be is a matter of conjecture which has exercised the minds of innumerable designers, market researchers and entrepreneurs since the debacle of the maxi skirt. We try to achieve a balance so that the strictures of technology and commerce do not stifle the creative spirit before it is strong enough to withstand and be enhanced rather than crushed by them.

By the mid-Seventies, St Martin's Fashion Department had become something of a creative power house and was ready to expand. We took stock of the Fashion world. Britain had joined the EEC. Designers were occupying important positions with big companies, some were running their own successful businesses while others had sunk, not through lack of talent but through ignorance of the financial realities of business. New professions had sprung up. Promotion was playing an increasingly important role in fashion. Fashion magazines, fashion pages in newspapers and colour supplements had become sophisticated, and visually exciting. Styling began to emerge as a recognisable activity. Increasingly production was taking place outside the UK and British fashion designers were going abroad to buy printed cloth, because they found it almost impossible to track down in Britain the kind of prints that would be good for clothes.

As a result of our observations, the newer one of our BA courses offers a choice of three areas for the students to specialise in: Fashion Design, Fashion Communicaton and Promotion, and Printed Textiles for Fashion.

Students who have opted to specialise in Fashion Design concentrate mainly on design, pattern cutting and sewing. If they wish, they may include knitwear or a small amount of printed textiles in their studies.

The Fashion Communication and Promotion group start writing, styling photographic sessions and some photography and typing. They continue with a reduced amount of fashion design and pattern cutting.

The group who specialise in Printed Textiles work mainly in the textile studio but also continue with some fashion design and pattern cutting. During the third year the students go out for their first taste of being employed. This can take place in the UK or abroad, and often is split into two or even three work experiences, so that the students are able to appreciate how different businesses operate.

The Fashion and Textile students' final year culminates in the production of a capsule collection which is shown at the St Martin's Summer BA Fashion Show. The Fashion Communication and Promotion students produce a complete dummy magazine tackling the advertising and the editorial sections and two other major projects of their own devising, which must include some really ambitious research such as a series of in depth interviews, a promotion campaign or a survey of a sector of the fashion market and this final work is presented as an exhibition to an invited audience.

MA students go on to extend their design and technical abilities, but we also wanted to teach them enough about business to make it feasible for us to demand that for their MA degree they show a collection of clothes or prints aimed at a particular market, and to support it by researching that market and presenting us with a feasibility proposal. To obtain first hand experience of team work, they work with the London College of Fashion technical students on special production projects. Both groups of students obtain great satisfaction from this exercise where the production students have their first taste of working with designers whose ideas they must try to understand and interpret and the designers have to learn how to communicate their designs clearly enough for someone else to produce a garment that will actually resemble their designs. The course culminates in the presentation of their collections at the St Martin's Winter MA Fashion Show.

We receive help from the fashion industry and several other colleges. The Polytechnic of Central London provides us with business studies, the London College of Fashion's language staff teach French and Italian to our students, and the

● Above, *Lumiere, winter 1984/85. Photo by Rob Cox.*

● Facing top left, *denim with sheepskin by John McKitterick for Levi's. Photo by Graham Murrell.*

● Facing top centre, *Jo Ballabriga coat in black/white giant herringbone, brilliant yellow lining with trompe l'oeil print of keys and Gauloises. And,* facing top right, *pale grey cotton trenchcoat. Photos by Graham Murrell.*

● Facing below left, *John Hopkins curry doeskin jacket, pale grey trousers, ecru knit sweater,* facing below centre, *coat in curry coloured facecloth and,* facing below right, *grey and brown plaid coat. Photos by Graham Murrell.*

production staff teach specialist production techniques. The London College of Printing organises a typing course for the Fashion Promotion and Communication group and the Derby Lonsdale College puts on an industrial knitting course for our MA knitters and the Cordwainer's College enables our students to make leather accessories. The fashion and textile industries of the UK, France, Italy and Japan have provided the students with unique work experiences.

The teaching at St Martin's is structured and the students work to briefs. Deadlines are set and must be met. While it is expected of the students to resolve the briefs in their own individual ways, work which fails to answer the brief is not acceptable. Completed work is pinned up on the studio walls, and each student's work is discussed – "critted" by the tutors before the whole group. This sounds, and at first is, horrendous, but a great deal can be learned from seeing how others resolve the same brief, and how they react to one's work. It is also a wonderfully desensitising process, anticipating the dreaded day when, inevitably, one must present work to potential employers.

A certain amount of healthy competition is encouraged, also initiative, efficiency and style. This is particularly true of the "making up projects" where the designs are taken through to garment stage and each student must present his or her work on a model of their own choosing, complete with make-up and accessories. For these "crits" we often invite a buyer or a journalist to add their comments to those of the design and technical tutors.

Since it is relatively easy for eminent but busy designers, journalists or PRs to come to us to set projects or give informal talks we are able to make maximum use of this invaluable pool of expertise. We also employ, as part-time tutors, a number of professional designers and journalists.

However, finally a college must also

● *Stephen Jones with hats. Photos for* Drapers Record *by Peter Paul (*top*) and Robert Erdmann (*above*).*

● Right, *satin slide by Benny Ong. Photo by Philip Webb.*

be a reflection of the staff who teach there all the time, and in that, St Martin's is fortunate in having a small but quite exceptional group of gifted teachers who possess the rare combination of being brilliant at their subject and also able to transmit some of this brilliance to their students, yet at the same time have the perception to discover whatever is special about a student and then the patience to develop it.

We encourage contact with the fashion world in all aspects and in many different locations. All the students help out at the London fashion events, and attend as many fashion shows and fashion and textile fairs as possible. Every student has at least one trip abroad, though most get hooked and save up, or use prize monies for a second or even third visit. The Fashion Design and Fashion Communication and Promotion students go to Paris or Milan and the Textile students to Milan and Como, or to Interstoff in Frankfurt. We have a student exchange arrangement with Parsons College in New York and each term one or two students go there for a three month stay.

A great variety of cults and fashions have, in fact, had their origins within the School. Masaru Amano's Assembly clothes, now renamed Steps and produced and marketed in Japan; Malcolm Taylor's tongue-in-cheek ecclesiastical mock baroque Romantics; Michael Sread's chic, crumpled, workwear linens; Corinne Drewery's Regency prints; Stephen Linard's Reluctant Emigrés in formal dress shirts made of organza, sheer enough to disclose the tattoos underneath; Darlajane Gilroy's elegantly studded punks; Richard Ostell's grommetted leathers; Tracy Wingrove's Hard Times family, complete with battered suitcase; Andrea Sargeant's and Mandy Taylor's patched and faded mendicants; Jo Ballabriga's witty, sexy, trompe-l'oeil clothes are a few that come to mind.

● *Steps: Masuru Amano's assembly knitwear. Crossover gilet with extra sleeves and belts.*

● *Extra Sleeves, to wear over/under sleeveless sweaters.*

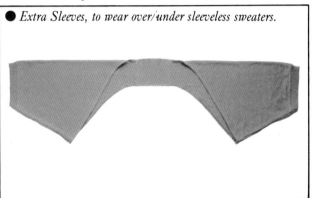

● *Belts and bandanas.*

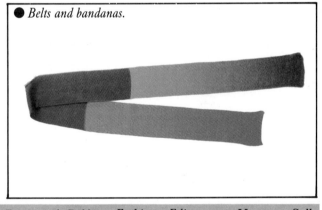

Many ex St Martin's students have made distinguished careers in fashion or textiles. To list them all would not fall far short of a telephone directory but a selection here has been made to indicate the variety of careers and locations.

The designers – in the UK: Katharine Hamnett, Benny Ong, Bruce Oldfield, Jacques Azagury, Willie Walters of Swanky Modes, Megumi Ohki of Lumière, Darlajane Gilroy, Richard Ostell, Dexter Wong, Tracy Wingrove of Wingrove & Leach, Annemaree Fitzgerald at Lana Lino, Mandy Taylor at Chelsea Girl and Tim Williams at Chelsea Man.

In France: Philip Waghorne at Lanvin, Alistair Blair at Karl Lagerfeld, Peter O'Brien at Chloé, Kathy Topham at Dior, Frank McEwan and Debbie Little at Cerutti, Frank Stevenson who has recently left Daniel Hechter to design for a Japanese company and Anthony Yong also ex-Daniel Hechter but now running his own highly successful international design studio.

In Italy: Keith Varty at Byblos, Liz Griffiths at Missoni, Marcus Biggs at Genny, Paul Harvey at UFO, Andrea Sargeant at Madonna, Penny Brooks at Iceberg, Michael Sread at Touche and Jo Ballabriga at Les Copains.

And in Japan: Masaru Amano and Stephen Linard.

The journalists – in the UK: Ann Boyd, Fashion Editor of The Sunday Times, *Kathy Phillips, Fashion Editor of* The Mail on Sunday, *Linda McLean,* Fashion Editor *at* Honey, *Sally Brampton, Fashion Editor of the* Observer, *Anne Drummond, Fashion Editor of* Girl about Town, *Ruth du Cann, Fashion Assistant at* Harpers & Queen, *Laura Hardy, Fashion Assistant at* Company.

And abroad: Liza Prangnell at Figaro Madame, *Paris, and Gladys Perint-Palmer at* San Francisco Magazine.

And the ones who don't fit into these categories: Mikel Rosen who produces fashion shows and promotions, Fizal Khan who works in Paris and Japan designing and forecasting, Maxi Si Wan who has become a stylist, John Babbage and Sue Byford who both work as fashion illustrators and Stephen Jones who has become the No. 1 hatter.

FAYRE TRADING

BLUE SWEET BLOOD, SWEAT,

and dry your tears. Percy Savage.

⬤ The Art of Promotion and the Promotion of Fashion is often a ménage
à trois involving three strange bedfellows: the producer, the promoter
and the public. The champions of the promotion of fashion are rare.
In London, three prime examples are still to the fore. Clare Rendlesham,
one-time fashion editor of *Queen*, has constantly and successfully promoted
both St Laurent for the Rive Gauche shops and Lagerfeld for the Chloé shop
in Bond Street.

As a result of the inevitable fashion earthquakes, Karl Lagerfeld transferred his affections and opened his own house with offices on the Champs Elysées and a showroom in New York on Fashion Avenue, once known as Seventh Avenue. The name was changed after years of lobbying by highly paid professional publicists and promoters and heavy-fisted businessmen, for fashion is big business. Lagerfeld means business and so does Lady Rendlesham. Off with the old and on with the new. Down with the Chloé shingle, and up with the newest name in Bond Street: Lagerfeld.

The second is Annette Worsley-Taylor, who has nurtured the London Designer Collections group for the past few years, until they finally ended up in the star position at the most beautiful exhibition ever seen at London's Olympia, The British Designer Show.

The third exceptional promoter of fashion is John Packer of the Scottish textile company Reid and Taylor. This hard-headed marketing man promotes his commodity – high quality textiles – through lavish promotions involving fashion designers from many countries. He has been organising events for the last 15 years, including a ball in a palace on the Grand Canal in Venice, a Leeds Castle fashion show and jousting tournament, and a ball in a grand schloss outside Munich. In 1983 at London's Guildhall, HRH The Duchess of Gloucester was his guest of honour and in Venice and Munich, HRH Princess Margaret was present. John Packer, the man behind all royal gloss was recently awarded the OBE, and an hour on the *Russell Harty Show*!

One of the prime examples of the promotion of fashion is the hard slog and the unending campaign waged by one of the sweatshop centres of today's world, Hong Kong. Their first notable success was in 1980 at the German fair, Igedo, held four times a year in Dusseldorf. Ann Chubb of *The Daily Telegraph* reported at the time that "... some 80 Hong Kong manufacturers represented the biggest ever group to show outside the tiny Crown Colony's confines." Part of the contingent were Jenny Lewis, an English designer based in Hong

● Above, *Prime Minister Margaret Thatcher was presented with a British Fashion Industry Award by Mr Cyril Kern, Chairman of Reldan, and Chairman of the British Fashion Council at a reception at No. 10 Downing St. in March 1984. Photo by Associated Press.*

● Above, *Madame Gres at 82 years of age, President of the Chambre Syndicale de la Haute Couture Parisienne, in her salon in the rue de la Paix. Photo by Cecil Beaton.*

Kong; Diane Freis, a Californian designer who had gone to Hong Kong in 1975 and was beginning to emerge as a name; Lim Ying Ying; Judy Mann and Eddie Lau. Eddie Lau according to Ann Chubb was, at the age of 29, the star of the Hong Kong designers at Igedo.

Freis was fortunate that she met Lady Tryon who so admired the versatility of her clothes that she began marketing them in England at the end of 1982 through her company, The Kanga Collection. Last season at Harrods, Diane Freis was one of the star designers. At the same time Lady Tryon opened her own shop in Beauchamp Place, after a launching party at the nearby San Lorenzo restaurant with royal friends and guests who included HRH Princess Margaret and The Duke and Duchess of Gloucester.

In 1981 Hong Kong organised a momentous exhibition in Paris at the Prêt-à-Porter. They opted for an entire hall and within those confines built one of the most beautifully designed trade exhibitions ever seen. The stand represented a fortified Chinese village, more in the manner of one of the palaces of the Forbidden City.

Le Figaro's fashion editor reported that the yellow peril's Trojan House would not win a war nor even a battle. But they certainly did impress the 50,000 odd visitors that season. Following the Paris success every trade exhibitor from London to New York, Milan to Munich tried to persuade the Hong Kong contingent to join their ventures, but a different tack was tried by The Hong Kong Development Council. They concentrated on store promotions.

The first was at Harvey Nichols in 1982 . . . that little temple of elegance whose wonderful windows are the envy of designers the world over. Indeed their windows carry messages comparable to hoardings on international urban roadsides.

Another of the world's major department stores and never slow to get any message was Harrods. What had been in effect a very attractive trial run at Harvey Nichols became a major reality at Harrods in 1984 with not only a vast amount of merch-

- Above left, *Lady Tryon and Lydia Dunn of the H.K.T.D.C. at Harrods. Photo by Richard Young.*

- Above right, *H.R.H. Princess Margaret and John Packer in Munich.*

- Centre, *a Diane Freis polyester-georgette from the Kanga Collection. Photo by Patrick Lichfield.*

Above, *Harvey Nichols Hong Kong window 1982.*

Top right, *New York designer Sao at Harrod's International Room.*

Far right, *Annette Worsley-Taylor and David Spanier of L.B.C. at Harvey Nichols.*

Right, *Pierre Berger, Zizi Jeanmaire and Yves St. Laurent at Diana Vreeland's Costume Institute opening in New York.*

Bottom left, *Marie Helvin, dressed by Bruce Oldfield, with Hugo Vickers at Harvey Nichols. Photos by Tracy Chamoun.*

Bottom right, *Andrew Wyles of Harvey Nichols with Elizabeth and David Emanuel.*

Centre, *St. Laurent's Haute Couture in Abraham silk. Photo by Claus Ohm.*

andise, but a massive advertising campaign, numerous colour pages in *The Times* and *The Standard* and the same in the London glossies – *The Tatler*, *Vogue* and *Harpers & Queen*.

Harrods laid out the red carpet for Hong Kong's biggest ever store promotion and millions of merry shoppers swept in to buy French cheeses and Italian wines, or delicious Moroccan oranges and Jaffa grapefruit, or even the Rosemary Turnbull design for Parigi, a leopard print two-piece in polyester georgette featured by Anne Price in her "Hooked on Hong Kong" article in *Country Life*, or perhaps one of the fabulous eight foot cloisonné vases at only £45,000 (the piece). "Oh no Sir, there are only two," the buyer told me when I asked. "I hope to God we didn't buy any more!"

At the same time as the Hong Kong Promotion was happening in London, the Milan trade fair and Igedo in Dusseldorf were held, followed in London by the immensely successful British Designer Show at Olympia, which culminated in a private and totally unpublicised visit by The Princess of Wales. The blue blood of British Fashion had the Royal Accolade. That trade fair was followed by the very successful exhibition in Harrogate.

Fashion is as much a commodity as a Prime Minister or a Papal Visit and in each instance top promoters and publicists are engaged for either their seasonal launches, political campaigns or Papal perambulations. "My Fer Lady" was the headline in one of France's leading publications following Mrs Thatcher's intransigent attitude at the Brussels Summit Meeting in March 1984. Only a couple of days later Mrs Thatcher received a selection of international store presidents and press at No. 10, Downing Street Martine Henno of *Le Figaro* reported that the "Dame de Fer" or the Iron Lady of Europe had opted for a velvet gown the evening of the reception.

As Annette Worsley-Taylor said, "On the night when the Prime Minister organised her reception, there were a lot of bruised egos among the London Fashion World personalities." Fortunately the hund-

reds of egos who had been only too glad to be both bruised and battered at the receptions organised in previous seasons were able to dry their tears and lick each other's wounded prides at the reception to which they were invited at Harvey Nichols by *Harpers & Queen* and The London Designer Collections. The cream of the pique assiette cream spent an eblouissante evening on the fifth floor of the store in an atmosphere of pure magic.

The international buyers and fashion press moved like swarming bees from Milan and Dusseldorf to London and thence to Paris.

In the spacious gardens of the Tuileries there is a huge round pond situated between the Obelisk of the Concorde at one end, and at the other end of the long alley, the beautiful little Triumphal Arc du Carrousel in the garden of the Louvre Museum. It is in this heavenly setting that the "Chambre Syndicale du Prêt-à-Porter des Couturiers et des Createurs de Mode" and the "Federation Française du Prêt-à-Porter Feminin", the two governing bodies of the French Fashion World have elected to combine their forces and participate in the ten-day-long marathon of one-man fashion shows which are held in four tents.

Entrance to the fashion shows is often only gained with a determination that a horde of migrating lemmings bent on suicide could not equal. Under idyllic conditions in the Tuileries this can sometimes be bearable but with a change of weather can come a change of mood. The scene can and did resemble a sad Bernard Buffet . . . stark, black, leafless trees with a myriad of black-clad, raven-like, look-alike, flapping androgynous forms, inverted umbrellas, drenched by the cold rains, slogging their way from tent to tent in the puddles of Tuileries mud.

During the March fashion shows, Thierry Mugler filled the Zenith, a huge rock concert complex at the Porte de la Villette on the outskirts of Paris. Fifty-five model girls showed 250 garments to an audience of 6,000.

While Mugler had taken over Thursday night, the highlight of Friday was the Diamonds Interna-

● Above, *Hubert de Givenchy preceded th launch of his new Ysatis perfume with a pres entation of his collection at the Guildhall i aid of The Save The Children Fund. Photo graphed with Madame Emmanuel de Marg erie, wife of the French Ambassador to th Court of St. James, Chairman of the organi sing committee, with H.R.H. Princess Anne Mrs Mark Phillips, GCVO, President of Th Save The Children Fund. Her Royal Highnes recently accepted to be Honary President of th British Knitting & Clothing Export Counci. Photo by Fritz Curzon.*

● Facing above, *two eminences grises of th international fashion world, Hebe Dorsey o the International Herald Tribune and Dian Vreeland of the Costume Institute at Ne York's Metropolitan Museum. Photo by Charlie Gerli.*

● Facing below, *two eminences grises of th international fashion world, John Fairchild o Fairchild Publications and Gustav Zumsteg o Abraham, without whose aid the St. Laurer Retrospective at the Costume Institute woul not have been possible. Photo by Charlie Gerl*

tional Awards Gala at the Musée des Monuments Français in the Palais de Chaillot. The 24 finalists included Barbara Tipple from Southsea in England. One of France's winning pieces, by Marie-Paule Quercy of Paris, was a necklace like the rim of an umbrella, dripping with diamonds. The magnificent display later moved to Basel to be exhibited at the annual European Watch, Clock and Jewellery Fair, the most important in Europe.

Under the aegis of Monsieur Mouclier and of Mademoiselle Dubois, the Chambre Syndicale have assiduously attacked overseas markets by taking along their highly professional troop of model girls to stage shows and have methodically gone to every overseas centre, first to North America, then on to the Far East circuit and are now prepared to tackle another potentially rich market – South America.

It must be remembered that whilst the message carried is one of French dressing, the results in business are more often than not seen in the increased sales of their accessories. And it is there that the French remain supreme – in the licensing of their prestigious names. They want blood!

It is surprising how few designers in England have brought out lines of accessories and successfully marketed them and gone from fame to fortune. The few who spring to mind are Mary Quant, the Emanuels, Zandra Rhodes and, of course, the royal dressmaker Hardy Amies.

Guided by Monsieur Lauriol, the French Federation du Prêt-à-Porter Feminin, who succeed admirably in luring the overseas buyer to the Porte de Versailles exhibitions, also practise a policy of expansion which has had remarkable results for continuing to fly the flag, French of course.

The French do more than any other nation to promote their industry both on French territory and overseas. Indeed they can be credited with over 60 exhibitions a year in 15 countries. In England, the French Clothing and Textile Centre, under the direction of Marie-France Brown organises the best of overseas shows seen in England. The "Touch of France" Exhibition is not only beautifully designed but is most careful of its quality of merchandise and just who is admitted to the exhibition. The Sweet Smell of Success is Sweat!

● *Marie-Paule Quercy won a 1984 Diamonds International Award for this design in a fine platinum mesh over a frame of yellow and white gold and sprinkled with pear-shaped diamonds.*

BLITZ
stylemagazine

Carey Labovitch · Simon Tesler

● There was a time when Fashion was for those who could afford it, and Fashion magazines were status symbols of wealth, taste and haute couture. But times have changed and Fashion, as we used to know it, has moved on faster than the seasons, almost faster than time itself, giving new life to, and rapidly becoming superceded by, another concept: Style. Not Style as it once was, a fashion accessory reflected in the way you crossed your legs or held a cigarette, but Style as an end all in itself.

STYLED BY IAIN R WEBB, PHOTOS BY MIKE OWEN.

The golden age of Punk brought fashion down from the catwalk to the level of the streets, taking the fashion magazines by surprise, allowing them to lag behind, and causing a distinct generation gap between the people who wrote about fashion, and the people who were wearing it in local high streets. Slow to catch on to this new sub-culture of self-styled independents, the fashion magazines began to lose their impact and value, finding it harder and harder with their long copy dates to keep up with the times.

Street fashion in Britain is world-renowned, probably more innovative, and certainly more versatile than in any other country. It's the product of circumstance: economic depression, unemployment, the joint influences of music and the media. It's a form of self-expression, and a mark of individuality; an outward sign of security, or the desire to be part of an elect tribe.

Of all the influences on British street fashion, music is the most powerful, and the only common denominator among young people. Where a couture house may take several months in which to establish the simplicity of a new hemline, a type of music can inspire a new fashion overnight.

Today, the fashionable flit from one band to another, constantly improvising; adopting and rejecting fashions within a week, while a new breed of young designers, fresh out of our art schools, wear down their heels on the teeming streets, setting new standards for an alternative haute couture.

Never before has there been so much activity, with fashion editors the world over turning their attention to the streets of London in particular, and to this plethora of bright new British designers.

● Right, *for his final year show at St Martin's School of Art, Simon Foxton's collection of menswear and sportswear was inspired by East End gangland ideology. Styling by Iain R Webb, Photos by David Hiscock.*

And the British fashion magazines have learned to cope, gradually, by marketing specific styles to their own select readership. For just as street fashion has become a product of rival splinter-groups, so the fashion magazines have had to adapt themselves by homing in on a particular segment of an infinitely fragmented market, becoming increasingly specialised in the process. The wide range of women's magazines, the main mouthpieces of fashion, have broken down readership rivalry by marketing not only to a particular type of woman, but to a specific age group and its tastes, and by signposting that market in the title of the magazine itself: *Just Seventeen, 19, Over 21.*

While magazines such as *Vogue* remain sole bastions of the haute couture market, new titles have emerged at the other and of the scale to cope specifically with street fashion, and old titles have adapted themselves to cater to this new and eclectic market.

But women's magazines and fashion magazines are no longer the only mouthpieces of fashion; the sudden diversity of fashion is reflected in the variety of press that now carry fashion pages – everything from the daily papers to the free local magazines that drop through the letterbox. But perhaps most interesting of all are the Lifestyle magazines which battled for supremacy in the Sixties before finally fading into the Sunday supplements, and which are only now beginning to re-emerge as important sounding-boards of Style.

For a certain class of person, or even a certain age group, magazines such as *The Tatler* and *Harpers & Queen* suggest a particular type of living and a particular style, and cost,

● Right, *Fashion at War: Iain R Webb translated the continuous battle of the trend-setting street tribes into his own "clothes for heroes", mixing the second-hand with the new. Photos by Mike Owen.*

of dressing. For the younger or more street-wise generation, youth culture magazines such as BLITZ have sprung up in the wake of the pop press, offering by way of editorial a cross-section of popular culture and media profile, with a mirror onto the lifestyles and fashion influences of readers. BLITZ readers are not only highly fashion-conscious, but style-conscious individuals, whose style of dress is only one facet of a way of life; a response to the multiple stimuli of popular culture, carefully selected and tailored by the individual to conform to a particular lifestyle. And that lifestyle is apparent in more than just clothes. BLITZ's coverage of the way people decorate their homes, or the kind of cars that they drive, is just as important as its fashion reportage.

For Style is not only what you wear, but how you wear it; the extra "found" items and accessories you carry with you, the way you walk or talk, even the type of music, or film, or book you like. Everything, in fact, that demonstrates what kind of person you are.

And so, as a lifestyle magazine and mirror onto youth culture, a magazine like BLITZ has to cater for a wide set of interests, from street and young designer fashion, to the social and media stimuli that influence youth culture. On the strict fashion front, it prefers to record rather than dictate, to offer ideas and capture images. The emphasis is always on the creative – not necessarily what can be bought, but how to transform the run-of-the-mill into the extraordinary. The emphasis of the magazine is also on the young and media-conscious, and it is of particular importance that the staff are of the same age group and interests as the readers.

● *The original idea behind these pictures was merely to present a selection of different types of glasses available through a new and trendy London optician. But as stylist Iain Webb and photographer Gill Campbell worked on the pictures something rather more exciting developed. There is after all no need to use garments as they were originally intended by the makers – the veils in this picture are a selection of army surplus scarves, and the cowl round the model's head in the picture opposite is actually an extremely pricey Giorgio Armani cardigan . . .*
(BLITZ no. 23, July/August 1984.)

Lifestyle magazines are a way of life in themselves, thinner versions of coffee table books, to be left lying about as symbols of a person's own lifestyle, a means of identification. They should not need to play upon the insecurities of their readers by promoting beautiful people in beautiful (and expensive) clothes as an ideal to which the reader should aspire. Instead, they serve a purpose in recording while informing: this is *you*; this might interest you; take a look at this person, isn't he a little like you? In a sense, they're a printed substitute for television, more compact and infinitely more portable. Their pictures may be static, but the class and quality of a stylish photograph can be just as important as the comments of a stylish person. You don't have to know *how* a person speaks, if the photographs themselves suggest mood and personality.

There was a time, a few years ago, when it was thought that video and television would outlive and even replace magazines. Yet more fashion/style magazines have been born over the last year than at any time since the Sixties, and the trend towards glossy pictorial records of the times in the form of magazines has grown beyond even the most optimistic of speculations. Fashion and Lifestyle magazines are here to stay, and the larger the choice, the more specialised they will become. For, in a word, they are now wholly and definitely *fashionable*.

● Right, *American-born Phyllis Cohen, the 24-year-old make-up artist extraordinaire, was commissioned to turn model Michaela into a Picasso. Photo by Mike Owen.*

FETISH FASHION

text and photographs
Ted Polhemus · Lynn Procter

1984 was a sort of fast-forward replay of the Swinging London phenomenon of the 1960s. British pop groups took over the world's charts, up and coming British designers and street stylists were recognised as a force to challenge any presumptions of haute couture dominance of the fashion business and it was cool to be kinky – fetishism was back in fashion.

Whereas for the Sixties this had meant Marianne Faithfull in black leather, Nancy Sinatra in kinky boots and Jane Fonda as Barbarella in see-through plastic, 1984 fetish fixation was mostly about rubber – a material which not that long ago seemed about as likely to attract the fashionable as, well, the day-glo fluorescent colours which also this year escaped from the Siberian wastelands of the un-hip.

But ... rubber? However did it come about that the stuff of wellingtons and washing up gloves made it into chic fashion shops from London to Tokyo, New York to Paris? As in any good detective story, the answers come from unexpected and disparate sources. In this case clues are to be

found in the world of interior design and architecture, in the hunger of post-punk musicians for a perversity fix and in the pressure cooker of London's ever changing club culture.

Firstly it was the school of high tech design which made rubber acceptable. Together with rough steel scaffolding, metal grids and all purpose trolleys, chunky industrial rubber floor coverings were recognised as acceptable materials for the home and office to be cherished and displayed by the high tech hipsters. As architecture, interior design and clothing are in a state of perpetual interface it was inevitable that as rubber evolved from floor coverings to table mats, someone somewhere would think of wearing

the stuff.

Jewellery was the first domain of fashion to fall to the high tech hordes. One designer started making rubber earrings and others followed with their own rubber jewellery experiments. Before long, however, not just jewellery but belts, handbags and other accessories were croping up with rubber trim and then garments began to appear with rubber bits where previously one would have found leather.

Although this was clearly more industrial chic than fetish fashion, the public reaction to the use of rubber in jewellery, accessories and clothing was inevitably mindful of fetishistic connotations.

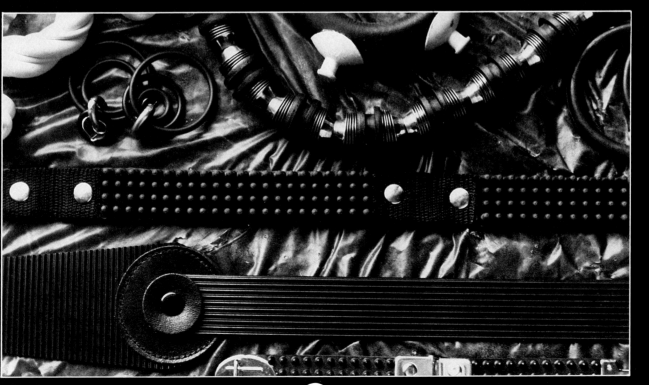

We had all seen Allen Jones's exploration of this area in his Sixties and Seventies paintings and sculptures. We had heard of the Mackintosh Society and other enclaves of enthusiasts who get off sexually on the stuff. And we knew that some of the original punk stylists such as Jordan and Vivenne Westwood of the "Sex" shop in the King's Road had employed rubber for its shock value. But although this aspect had been excluded from the Seventies fashionalisation of punk by designers such as Zandra Rhodes, in 1984 even a super functional high tech aesthetic couldn't, when rubber was employed, overcome the erotic and fetishistic implications. There was simply no getting around the fact that because leather and PVC had, since the Sixties, been drawn into the fashion mainstream, rubber had been left alone to carry the can of fetishistic symbolism.

The process was helped along when pop people such as Marc Almond of Soft Cell and Genesis P Orridge of Psychic TV began a reappraisal of punk's exploration of hard core fetishism. "Porno Sleaze" was what Almond called it and he enthused in interviews about the latest Centurians catalogue from the States which featured rubber and other fetishistic paraphernalia while Soft Cell's banned *Non-Stop Erotic Cabaret* video explored every area of sexuality which was sufficiently alternative. This all dovetailed with the goings on at the Batcave club – which is run by members of the band Specimen – and sexual perversity in just about any

● Previous Page, *a selection of jewellery and belts from Detail which celebrate high tech aesthetic and industrial origins.*

116

form became trendy in certain pop/club circles. Rubber fetishism was a part of this but leather too was yanked back out of the acceptable fashion mainstream and restyled into garments explicitly derived from the world of true fetishism.

The gay world had, of course already explored this sort of thing and in 1984 it finally emerged onto the pop scene when Frankie Goes to Hollywood's *Relax* became a number 1 hit despite being banned by the BBC. But what was interesting about the Soft Cell/Specimen tread was that it got sexual perversity out of the gay ghetto. And as the Batcave became *the* place to go and bands rushed to get onto the pop sleaze bandwagon, the door was opened for fetish fashion to escape onto a still largely unsuspecting populace.

Then, in January 1983, a club called Skin 2 opened in London's Soho. The first nights saw pop people like Almond and Siouxsie mingling with rubber enthusiasts from the Mackintosh Society and dominatrices from suburbia clad in leather and studs. Suddenly the leap had been made from all purpose polymorphous perversity to explicit fetishism.

For lifelong enthusiasts of rubber leather, PVC, bondage, discipline and such like, Skin 2 marked the first time since the Sixties that they could come out of the closet. Such people had for years been buying their private apparel from firms such as Sealwear of Bournemouth who specialise in rubberwear and Atomage of London the leather and PVC couturiers. Atomage's beautifully made and very

● Left, *Johnny Melton of Specimen – the band which founded and runs the Batcave, one of London's most influential clubs – dressed in a black rubber catsuit overlaid with ripped fishnet and trimmed with maribou at the wrists and ankles designed by Theresa Coburn.*

● Above, *black leather dress from Ya Ya in Kensington Market.*

● Left, *John Sutcliffe started designing tight fitting "protective" garments back in 1947, originally for motorists. Before long he gave up his job repairing china to set up the Atomage company which still specialises in custom made leather and PVC outfits. Left, a 1972 catsuit, mask, boots and gloves. Atomage's garments are much admired by the Skin 2 crowd but few can afford to buy these hand made garments. Photo by John Sutcliffe.*

● Above, *PVC corset and gloves from She-an-me, a firm which has for many years supplied pop stars, punks and the Hot Gossip dancers as well as the usual buyers of "glamour wear". The fact that She-an-me's garments had previously had a lot of media exposure meant that they were too passé for most of the Skin 2 trendsetters, which left rubber as the one fetishistic material which still maintained its shock value.*

● *The opening night of London's Skin 2 club saw full fledged fetishists who had waited all their lives for a chance to go public mingling with the established crowd whose only fetish is fashion and the shock of the new. Below right, leather dresses and whips. Above right, rubber and lycra mask, top hat and rubber coat.*

● *The Sealwear company of Bournemouth has been making garments for rubber enthusiasts for many years. A few of Skin 2's founder members went there in good time to have exotic outfits made for the club's opening night but the fashionable crowd who came to the club and admired garments like these didn't like the idea of waiting weeks for delivery and wanted up to the minute designs – thus was fetish fashion born. Centre right, pink and lilac rubber nurse's outfit from Sealwear.*

expensive leather cat suits had become famous in the Sixties as attire for the early *Avengers* TV show but in the Seventies things had returned to normal, to the business of quietly catering for a minority of enthusiasts of "restrictive" and "protective" garments, the true fetishists whose attraction to rubber, leather and bizarre styles is a personal taste which pays no attention to fashion and may in some cases become an obsession which few can understand.

Anthropologists first used the term fetish to describe objects possessing a magical power. Voodoo dolls and such like are probably the best known examples of these fetishes but anything, including natural objects such as stones and bits of bone, can serve such a purpose. The important thing is that the object is presumed to have a power above and beyond that which would normally be expected. More recently psychologists have used the term fetish to describe objects, materials or even bits of the human body, like feet, which exercise a sexual power over certain individuals. Some complicated and some frankly far fetched theories have been put forth to explain fetishistic obsessions but in essence these all boil down to the fact that a kind of imprinting can occur in human development whereby sexual desires become linked to and dependent upon objects which are not normally seen as especially erotic. The way in which this happens seems to be the result of chance associations between an individual's early sexual development and the presence of particular objects and

● *Not just rubber but all sorts of fetishistic garments became fashionable in 1984. For example, the oldest fetish of all, the corset, was revived in classic as well as new experimental forms. Right,* a wasp-waisted effect is created by using a tightly buckled lace trimmed belt over a taffeta halter top and skirt with peplum designed by Laurie Vanian for Symphony of Shadows in Hyper Hyper.

suddenly become fashionable, even if it is still very much a minority style.

That fetishism itself should become fashionable is less of a surprise. Fashion is a hungry machine which, because of its raison d'être of systematic, perpetual change, is in constant need of new ideas so that this season's look can be readily seen as different from previous years' looks. To this end we have seen all sorts of traditional folk costumes – from Peruvian peasant styles to Japanese workwear to industrial overalls to African prints fashionalised for a season and then discarded when the shock of the new begins to pale. Fetishistic garments are also anti-fashions; like the dress of peasant communities, stockings and suspenders, corsets, stilettos, etc, are traditional garments which derive significance from the fact that they are seen as changeless.

The fashionalised fetishes are therefore obviously not true fetishes and the people who adopted them in 1984 are obviously not true fetishists. What happened at Skin 2 was that London's fashionable club goers, who were used to being the sartorial centres of attention, found themselves in a situation where they looked drab and normal in comparison to the exotic costumes of established enthusiasts from the suburbs and the provinces.

These trendy, would-be fashion fetishists were much impressed with the traditional rubber wear but, knowing that the fashion world they inhabit is too fast changing for them to wait weeks for a garment to be

● Right, *black corset dress from Symphony of Shadows in Hyper Hyper.*

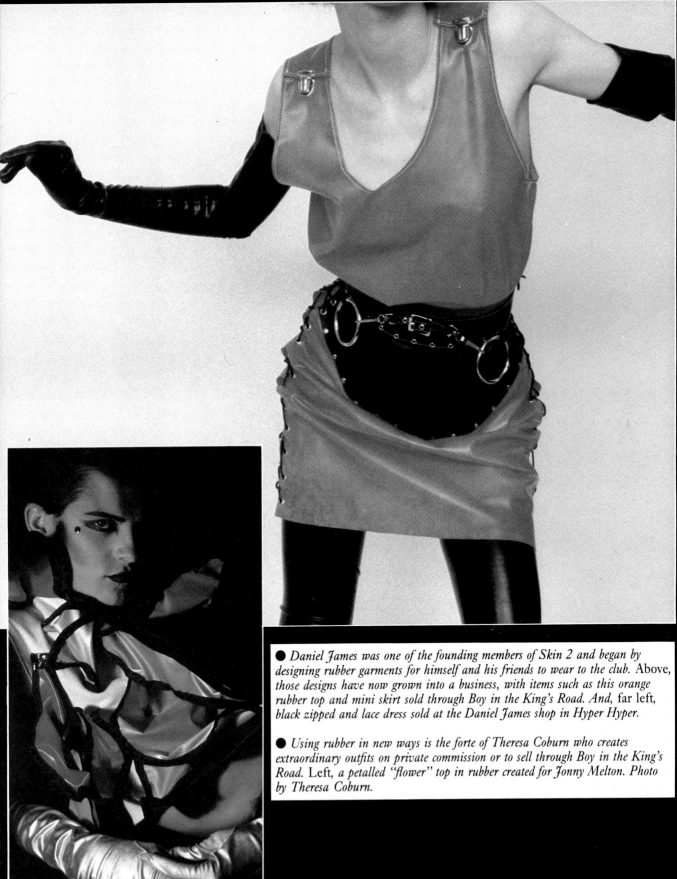

● Daniel James was one of the founding members of Skin 2 and began by designing rubber garments for himself and his friends to wear to the club. Above, those designs have now grown into a business, with items such as this orange rubber top and mini skirt sold through Boy in the King's Road. And, far left, black zipped and lace dress sold at the Daniel James shop in Hyper Hyper.

● Using rubber in new ways is the forte of Theresa Coburn who creates extraordinary outfits on private commission or to sell through Boy in the King's Road. Left, a petalled "flower" top in rubber created for Jonny Melton. Photo by Theresa Coburn.

made to measure by an established mail order firm, they set about designing things themselves. Initially the object was just to have something one step ahead to wear at the club and clothing was sold through the "Where did you get that dress? Do you think your friend would make one for me?" system. But soon stalls in Kensington Market, Hyper Hyper in Kensington and the shop Boy in the King's Road were stocking some fetish fashions in rubber as well as PVC and leather. And as the world's fashion industry was in 1984 keeping a sharp eye on London, what had started in a small club in Soho proceeded to spread world wide.

But while in London at Skin 2 one could see the trendy fashion fetishists dancing side by side with true fetishists who had been waiting all their lives for the chance to come out of the closet about their obsession with rubber, leather, PVC or whatever, outside London – as far afield as New York and Tokyo where the fetish fashion designers were discovering new markets for their ideas – there was no opportunity to juxtapose the real thing and the trendy immitation.

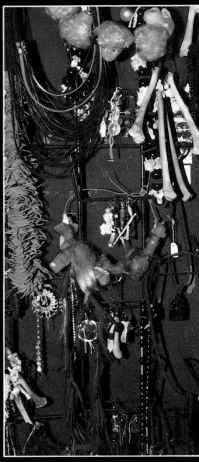

● *Rubber garments were much in
evidence at the 1984 Olympia Fashion
Fair where foreign buyers overcame
their initial shock and got out their
order books.* Right, *rubber blouse and
skirt and rubber dress by G-Force
available from New Masters in Hyper
Hyper and from the G-Force shop in
Nottingham.* Far right, *rubber dress
and overcoat by Barbara de Vries for
Giraf.*

● *Rubber jewellery has now moved
on from early high tech and industrial
influences and has developed into
overtly fetishistic forms.* Above, *a
display of necklaces and earrings in
rubber and other materials at Fetisch
Or Die, Kensington Market.*
Overleaf, *bracelets by Tom Binns
available from Detail.*

One cannot help but wonder what a middle aged fetishist couple from Ohio might make of it all – but then what would Chairman Mao or Nehru have made of the fashionalisation of their jackets? Some fetishist purists such as the Mackintosh Society have chosen to stay away from Skin 2 but many enthusiasts have been thrilled to discover how a younger generation has adopted and adapted as fashion that which they were often too involved with to contemplate improving on.

And where will it all end? The true fetishists will go on being into whatever it is they are into but by next year the fashionable will undoubtedly have moved on; for them the only fetish is fashion itself. Probably the only long term effect will be the rehabilitation of rubber as a legitimate material for fashion designs and clothing manufacturers to use. Rubber should now take its place alongside silk, leather, lycra, fur, cotton, nylon and all the other fabrics we use today. Like leather, which only a few years ago was simply not respectable, rubber may now provide new possibilities and inspiration for high fashion designers and street stylists alike.

'If I don't get those cha-cha heels...'
THE FRONTIER ETHIC OF anti-fashion

● *Speak, follicle! When Annie Lennox (right) borrowed the Brilliantine backroll of pop culture's most famous icon, she* *was trying to turn reflected stardom back into modern style.* TINTS: TONY STEWART.

Though the dictionary defines it as "the prevailing customs and usages of upper-class society, especially in dress", *fashion* is really a way to re-spell *thievery*. It is also a code-word for industry: formidable energies are expended each year on convincing an insecure public that identity can be visually conferred upon them in exchange for cash.

text: CYNTHIA ROSE   design: TONY STEWART

As ex-*Women's Wear Daily* high sheriff James Brady put it, fashion is "also the rich and glamorous who buy the clothes and set the trends; the rich husbands who paid for the clothes; the slim young men who cuckold those husbands; the restaurants, the galleries, the resorts and the houses where "the" clothes are worn. Fashion is more than the clothes. It is also the spirit which goes into their creation, the money – sometimes very large money – that is involved in their distribution and the people who wore the clothes or were worn by them".

Corporately speaking, Brady remains correct ten years later. But the 1980s have fostered additional confusion between matters of celebrity and matters of consequence; the entire climate of today trains the public to place their trust in merchants and in the media, rather than directing their interest towards personal, spontaneous preference.

Allusion, not reality, is after all the stock-in-trade of fashion – which must remain relentlessly seasonal. Even people who do not "follow" couture eventually become familiar with the name designers' *Great Gatsby* or *Brideshead Revisited* phases via the indulgence of the famous or the filtering-down of knock-off versions.

And the more famous the clotheshorse, the greater currency a look accrues, outstripping its actual source through sheer exposure. How many fastidious Teddy boys figure that Elvis Presley's "personal image" – which preceded his music by some years – was possibly due to the movie of a pulp novel starring Tony Curtis? The flick was 1949's *Across the River*, a translation to celluloid of Irving Shulman's *The Amboy Dukes* which featured Curtis as anti-hero/protagonist Frank. Speculation arose when Elvis dashed out for a "Tony Curtis cut" (which everyone else around him referred to as a DA) after Curtis had just caused a sensation in what was only his second screen role.

What was the outward image of an Amboy Duke – a Jewish juvenile delinquent whose gang took its name from Amboy Street – which might have struck a chord in Presley? "The first and most lasting impression of Frank's appearance," read Shulman's

original novel, "was one of sullenness. His face was a bitter challenge – a pugnacious invitation to an attempt to kick him ... the hardness of muscle and bone which is the heritage of those who do not succumb to the threadbareness of poverty." Whether directly affected by this or not, Elvis passed *his* version of the image into pop iconography so effectively that in 1984 Annie Lennox can still create a sensation collecting a music industry award on television costumed as the Big E himself.

So who does the industry of artifice really feed from? Ironically, not the conquered hordes but those who constitute the exceptions to its rules. Designers, merchandisers, fashion journalists and publicists hover as piranha around any nascent cult, movement or artistic avant-garde – in hopes of scavenging raw material for another "look".

The production of visual novelty about their persons is not the sole business of artists, writers, performers and film-makers; their chief interest can consist of extrapolating from direct experience some idea of meaning communicable to others. Personal appearance may constitute merely part of the pleasure in their lives (or, in showbiz, part of the professional territory).

Fashion sells clothes but real artists – for better and worse – work out visions. It is when these visions achieve notice that the fashion vultures of the Eighties begin to buzz about the headiness of their 3-D existence before dishing up a palatable, reductionist version.

Architects of style may also aim for or achieve status of their own, for the fashion industry owes obeisance to anyone who manages to re-define the desirable in the minds and eyes of the buying public. Robert Mapplethorpe became a celebrity in the fashion world because of the *way* in which he photographed celebrities. With his *GQ* cover shots and this year's glossy book of beefcake portraits, Bruce Weber has surpassed Mapplethorpe for broad-spectrum influence: his Olympic hopefuls and strapping teen idols decree a new, post-Dean genre of blue-collar hunk.

The work which first made Weber

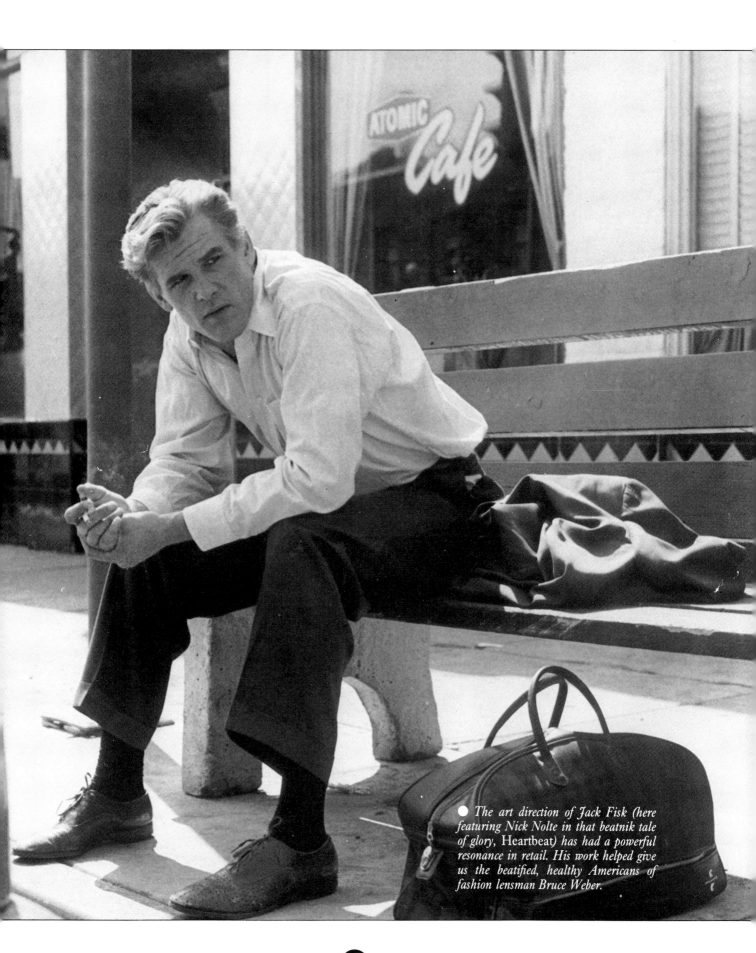

● *The art direction of Jack Fisk (here featuring Nick Nolte in that beatnik tale of glory, Heartbeat) has had a powerful resonance in retail. His work helped give us the beatified, healthy Americans of fashion lensman Bruce Weber.*

● *Punk had neon poetry of colour and clamour – but the rhinestone romance of a new frontier really does hide a heart of gold. Jason Ringenberg's pistol tie helps fashion "revolve".*

PHOTOS: PETER ANDERSON.

a mainstream image-monger was the *Vogue* fashion spread "Pioneers of 82", an atmospheric jumble of vignettes romanticising life on the plains of the US when her West was still to be won. Shot on location in Nebraska, the photo-spreads were technically tied to the re-publication of Willa Cather's *oeuvre* by Virago Books that same autumn. Yet their ambience was clearly a throwback to the art direction of the talented Jack Fisk (*Heart Beat, Raggedy Man*) on Terrence Malick's 1978 *Days of Heaven*, as well as the largely-unseen *Heaven's Gate* (1980).

Bruce Weber continues to promote the clean and clear-eyed image of ordinary Americans beatified, whatever his period, setting or props. And, to a society increasingly infatuated with an ideal of bodily health, his images have appeared more and more chic.

At the same time one very public art – popular music – is seeing a real folk revival, genuinely suffused by the conflicting loyalties, losses and sundered community inherited from the pioneers Weber's *Vogue* spread evoked. Probably the greatest public encouragement this movement received also occurred in Autumn, 1982, when the most popular white vocalist in America surprised his public with an acoustic album about the changes in that psychological geography within which Cather once wrote. The artist was Bruce Springsteen, the album's title *Nebraska*.

New, unashamedly patriotic bands – like Rank & File, Los Lobos, Jason and the Scorchers, Last Roundup, X, the Blasters and Lone Justice – wear what they have inherited, onstage and off. Stetsons, high-collar shirts, waistcoats, pearl-button cowboy duds, scarves, boots, stringpost ties and bandannas represent both the affectations of Hollywood's West from Gene Autry back through Hank Williams Nudie **Extravaganzas** *and* a fervent reclamation of that community ideal which lapsed into Nashville ritz.

One topic much of the work preaches *against* is fashion for fashion's sake. "It's a new order," says Tony Kinman, founder of Rank & File, a band which feeds left-wing lyricism and punk speed into highly traditional country sound. "We're into this because it's a means of expression at which we've arrived. We are part of today's country music just like we're part of today's country. It's no fad."

Inevitably, the successful end of the this multi-faceted musical movement has rubbed shoulders with the monolith that is the Country and Western image industry. Thus, it has also touched base with C&W's traditional audience (blue-collar workers, lower-income or disenfranchised whites, a substantial number of America's Hispanic and black populations) as well as with its own youthful contemporaries. Flanked by established "blue-collar rock" stars such as Springsteen or Tom Petty and newly visible Hispanic acts like Los Lobos, this change in popular music has also managed to reinstate some concern for both romance and religion in young lives.

Take Los Angeles' highly visible band X. Frequent television guests over the past year, their most recent album topped many an American magazine's year-end poll, and they re-recorded the title tune for a cheeky re-make of Godard's *Breathless* which starred Richard Gere. X has one female vocalist, Exene Cervenka. She has been widely cited as a fashion

● *Cyndi Lauper makes hay out of the straws which have broken other female singers' backs: on her own she carries a tradition of inventive sass determined to eschew class.* TINT: TONY STEWART.

influence ever since 1977, when the band emerged from a local "punk" scene under the patronage of Sixties superstar Ray Manzarek.

Exene's initial appearance – short dark hair and heavy makeup worn with thriftshop dresses – suggested a doom-stricken romantic heroine from the flickering silent screen. But in reality, as passing time and increasing fame have revealed, this full-busted, square-jawed lady (a published poetess who hails from Illinois) likes to decorate her body as she does her daily journals: for personal enjoyment. At one concert she will pair an off-

meaningful: they contain pictures of bikers and Jesus, decals of states traversed on tour, cocktail napkins and souvenirs, sketches of go-go girls, lingerie samples and lucky poker cards. "All these things illustrate my life," claims Cervenka, who married her composing partner and stage partner John Doe in Tijuana on Easter Day, 1980.

John and Exene claim that marriage was for them an act of romantic *rebellion*, and both other (male) members of their band are wedded too. Order and moral commitment, concedes Cervenka, do not come easily today (a

his gimme hats, cowboy shirts, dog-tags, flashy oil-rigger's signet rings and post-performance cigars. And, like the music X make the households of its members are cluttered with both religious and pop cultural debris.

Exene feels no desire to be "credited" for any influence in fashion (her sister Mary had even more of an effect on avant-garde dress in Los Angeles until her untimely death in a car crash). "None of us cares about fashion. Fashion never gives credit anyway – it's all about taking someone else's imagination and trying to sell it to people with nothing of their own. We have something of our own – and we do it for enjoyment."

The West Coast music scene in which X evolved exploded into greater retail resonance through mega-selling groups like the GoGos and solo artists such as the cartoon-conscious Cyndi Lauper. All these girls carry on an American tradition of assimilation dressing – thrift shop+pastiche+ trende=costume – which dates back in time to the era of Edie Sedgwick. (An era resuscitated just recently by the first collection of pop star Debbie Harry's former personal couturier, Stephen Sprouse.)

Largely a white suburban phenomenon, the knack for pairing tutus and pedal pushers, beaded cardies and costume jewellery surfaced into an unofficial tradition as soon as the iron rules of Fifties conformity were shattered by the original beatniks. Betsey Johnson's Paraphernalia mini-skirts (patronised so publicly by the Warhol set) are not unrelated to Exene's nose-ring, stacks of bangles and layers of skirting, GoGo Belinda Carlisle's cheerleader-on-the-make stagewear, or the cross between beachwear and ballgown flaunted by Cyndi Lauper on American television.

In the mid-Eighties, such fun – independent of fashion's Hitlers, the designers and stockists – represents one facet of female assertiveness. Such women value their own taste; for them, glamour decreed by social pressure is a matter for museums. Or perhaps for galleries who follow the lead of Ronald Feldman's May 84 "show", *Socialites and Satellites*. Feldman's display encouraged viewers to see the clothing as political, as an

● *Spurred on to a new height in cowboy chic, two of Jason And The Scorchers show how the West was won.* PHOTO: PETER ANDERSON.

the-shoulder black velvet cocktail sheath with a leopardskin cowboy hat; at another, she will stack up two or three tatty tee shirts and top them with flashy jewels – including perhaps a paste tiara.

Exene's journals and scrapbooks reveal a Joseph Cornell absorption of images as physical, powerful and

tattoo over John's breast reads "EXENE", while his wife's arm spells *Temptation*). "But taking care of people you love is basic and natural," Doe insists, "whether or not there is any justice in the world."

John Doe lives up to his self-imposed all-American *soubriquet*, even if he does mix bangle bracelets with

● *Poetess, fringe film star and rock frontwoman, Exene Cervenka shuffles all the imageries of America – old and new, sacred and profane – in her wardrobe as well as her work. Why? "Plea-sure . . . convenience . . . work . . . delight!"*
PHOTO: DAVID ARNOFF.

extension of the social "obligations" of its day (the Fifties). *Socialites* offered an interpretation of how our past was clad rather than a Diana Vreeland-like exclamation over it.

Another personality with a high profile in the fashion media at the moment is New York writer Kathy Acker, a longtime survivor of Manhattan's avant-le-Polaroid art world circuit. Acker reiterates the "personal pleasure" rationale for home-made couture, although she often sets fashion references side by side with economic critiques in her meticulous prose.

Usually this takes the form of a sentence such as: "At a corner outside the huge windows of a nearby restaurant, two bums men between the ages of 30 and 50 who're wearing Issey Miyake clothing which doesn't cost a fortune, eye a Con Edison vehicle." Acker herself would not scorn a piece by Miyake, but the piled-laundry look she favours is a cheaper, more personal construction offset by her tufted, almost-shaven head, linen and leather accoutrements, numerous earrings (both studs and dangling talismans) and metal front tooth. The same look can also be deconstructed. . . . Acker likes to balance her sedentary occupation of writing with weight-lifting and sometimes incorporates her training clothes into her streetwear: leotards and short athletic boots for comfort, scarves and fetishistic jewellery for drama. Like Exene, whom she admires, Kathy leaves a very female lipstick trace on her tea and coffee cups.

Of course the men aren't about to get left out of the action: not when D-I-Y fashion can create showbiz fizz rather than the other way round. And the chief iconoclasts-come-lately have been black – street kids and rap teams, overshadowed in the main-

● Socialites & Satellites: *Ronald Feldman Fine Arts mounted a May '84 exhibition which re-viewed the politics as well as the panache inherent in Fifties clothing.* PHOTO: D JAMES DEE.

stream by a show-biz trio from the popular music front: Prince, Rick James and Michael Jackson.

James presents an outright caricature of conspicuous consumption refined from funkateer George Clinton before him (and extended into insulting cartoonery via American televison's "Mr T"). And Prince – with female sidekicks Vanity Six and creations the Mary Jane Girls – has simply married the costume kinks of gay chic and best-selling Heavy Metal music to the traditional theatricality of the black showbusiness scene.

Michael Jackson, however, is an altogether different phenomenon. As Exene Cervenka puts it, he is the "Jackie O of our age". The former First Lady moulded the Kennedys into cultural monarchs but Jackson has superseded even his mentor/idol as the living equation of superstardom and super-*power*.

The attention won by females as varied as the GoGos, Exene Cervenka and Kathy Acker shares one heartening aspect: all enjoy body shapes which have not been made to conform to any fashionable vision, yet

fashion's hawks have been careful to keep their attire in sight. (A spry, self-mocking film such as *Valley Girl* shows a provincial version of the GoGos hitting the mall racks – as the plot mixes pop, punk, imagination and romance with the "Valspeak" variant of teen slang.)

Yet those male performers – all black – who are breaking the greatest amount of new ground and enjoying the hottest media quotient showcase an ironic opposite. Led by the absolutely anorexic Jackson, their blitz of glitz allows for no "normality" at all. The more fame Jackson has accrued, the more he has refined his rock royalty pose; what began with classy casual wear – white socks, white suits, cashmere sweaters – required first cosmetic surgery and now an ever-present badge of status. (Elaborate brooches or sets of rhinestone pendants grace each of Michael's sweaters like military accolades; the uniform jackets which top his "man of the people" blue jeans have become progressively more encrusted with sequins and braid, epaulets and draped cords.)

Consistently representing himself as supra-human on video, Jackson has achieved dominance over a kingdom which knows no order of sexual preference or age. And when he made the cover of *Time* magazine via a Warhol portrait, the whizzkid was presented as a white man (almost certainly a joke at his expense by the portraitist, but conceivably Jackson's own wish).

Yet it was when designer Danny Whitten filled Jackson's request for six rhinestone-covered gloves – two black, one red-white-and-blue and the others white – so he need "never be offstage" that Jackson's youngest constituents suddenly went public. No sooner did one picture of the entertainer appear thus accessorised than even young black migrant workers' kids suddenly showed up at work wearing single white gloves in imitation: some net, some grotesquely outsize, some fingerless. The theatrical talisman's popularity brought to a head an already-extant controversy in the New York City school system – where phalanxes of "unorthodox" dressers were already defending their right to attend clad in

● *Fate sealed with a squeal: the leading lady of John Carpenter's* Christine *is, literally, the* Fury *of a sexy female (in this case a female* Plymouth Fury) *scorned.*

● *Michael Jackson – the singer who would be king – takes a uniform approach to the role of celebrity, and peppers his style.*

● *Kathy Acker uses clothes as she does prose – a pinch of plagiarism, a touch of posh and layers of irony.*
PHOTO: ROBERT MAPPLETHORPE.

the studded belts and unlaced sneakers popular from Jackson's videos. As "fashion" per se it didn't seem to matter so much – until suddenly watches bearing Michael's face were outselling their street competition from Rolex and retailers started to merchandise gloves separately: one for the price of two. As a statement of Jackson's control and influence over both audio and visual media, the white glove phenomenon could not say more.

We out here in the dark may still be struggling to assimilate the "meaning" of Michael Jackson's appearance (though a Jackson look-alike who popped up as a pimp in American television's 1984 re-make of *Mike Hammer* speaks for one segment of Hollywood). But previous icons whose visual identities *have* stabilised in the pantheon of fame also remain touchstones today; revival fashion is an industry in itself.

It too seeps on to cinema screens as blatant iconography, implicitly packing a codified "message" to film audiences. John Carpenter's *Christine*, for instance, spins a metaphoric tale

of sex as the bottom-line anarchy vital to rock and roll – yet does so within a *movie* format. Christine, a gleamingly red 1958 Plymouth Fury, is the film's leading lady. But its protagonist is her victim: a below-average schmo named Arnie who bears a striking resemblance to Buddy Holly.

Once hooked on Christine's fatal fuel (the real 1950s rock and roll her radio dispenses), however, it's all downhill for Arnie. Before the viewer knows it, he turns round to spit out something surly towards a local cop and whammo!, the viewer is looking at Private Elvis. The sneer, the arrogance, the turned-up velveteen collar in deep red – the corruption inherent in the contradictions which made the music that followed Holly genuinely dangerous and disruptive – magically appear before us. *Christine*'s creators have drawn on the auras and subtleties of both rock and memory to comment not just upon them but, more centrally, on sexuality and its expression.

Danger, disruptions, pleasure, person-hood. These are the sources from which "fashion" flows – only

fashion ossifies even as it succeeds in selling. It feeds on that popular art described so well by Claes Oldenburg in his 1961 *Store Days* manifesto. ("I am for an art that embroils itself with the everyday crap and still comes out on top... I am for an art that a kid licks after peeling away the wrapper... I am for an art that sheds hair... I am for the blinking arts, lighting up the night. I am for art falling, splashing, wiggling, going on and off.") But fashion petrifies that reality, that expression of experience, into a static parody – rather like Oldenburg's own *Lingerie Counter*, produced a year after his fiery declaration.

So this year avant-garde fashion ponders what can be extracted from Acker's anarchy, Exene's poetic womanhood, the pop titillations of Prince, the goldmine that lies whichever way Michael Jackson points his white glove. But fashion does not ask what is to be *done* out in the world where art sheds its hair, splashes, wriggles, and lights up the night. That more important question is – luckily – left for us.

AU SUZY

Conny Jude

a Portfolio

Symphony of Shadows

RUBBERISED
X X
X X

Daniel James Designs

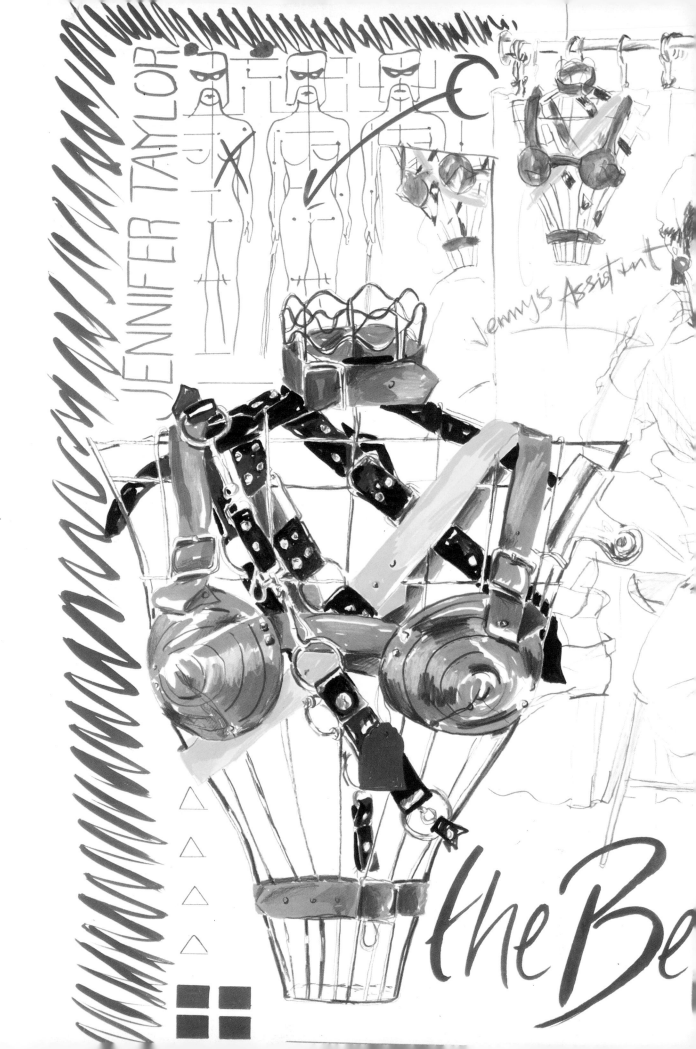

JENNIFER TAYLOR

Jennys Assistant

the Be

DAYGLO RHINESTONE
CRAZIES RENTBOYS
AND THE GLITTERGANG

Fiona Russell Powell

⬤ Just when it looked as if London's youth had, for the first time in eight years, lost inspiration and the street had been swept bare of ideas, the answer came along in the most unlikely form ever – the Glam Rock revival. Who would have thought that the current Glam-Retro look spearheaded by pop-stars like Annie Lennox of The Eurythmics and Boy George of Culture Club, both of whom were '77 punks, would now be sporting the clothes that most offended the sensibilities of original punk couture.

Annie Lennox posed recently in a gold lamé suit and platforms and the original Culture Club look – billowing tops, baggy trousers, all covered in Hebrew lettering and designed by Sue Clowes, has long since gone. Boy George has adopted and *adapted* the satin, glitter and tartan trademarks of early Seventies glam rock.

Pool together the look of The Sweet (once described as "a riot of glitter, satin and mascara"), Slade (who wore multi-coloured braces and huge platform boots), Gary Glitter (the King of Glam rock who owned an enormous wardrobe of expensive, custom-made glitter suits), and even David Bowie, who became the ultimate transsexual god when he appeared as the Starman on *Top of the Pops* in 1972, and one can trace the sources of inspiration behind the new look Boy George, who, twelve years later, is seen as the "ultimate transsexual god" by millions of adoring fans all over the world. A brief glance at the picture cover for Culture Club's April hit *It's a Miracle* will prove this. George is wearing a pair of World's End platform trainers, Bay City Roller-style tartan trousers, a blue and silver glittery kimono and a silver straw hat. He is holding a silver star-shaped guitar similar to the one played by Rob Davies of Mud, and wearing a pair of black, wet-look gloves with large diamanté rings worn *over* the gloves, just as Alvin Stardust did, circa 1974, when he had a hit with *My Coo Ca Choo*.

Over the past year, Boy George has insidiously introduced the idea of men wearing skirts and dresses to the British public. "Gender Benders" has been one of the most debated topics in the national press, now Boy George has become a National Institution with talk of his being awarded an MBE for services to the country. George is responsible for the band's image, dressing the rest of Culture Club in American baseball gear – sweatshirts with huge padded shoulders, tracksuit bottoms and lace-up Adidas and Pony trainers. George moved from a large stars-and-stripes coat worn with an oversize straw top-hat with extra frill to the Egyptian head-dress look within a month. He has gradually replaced the false dread-locks with his own hair which has been carefully coiffured into an extremely feminine Joan Collins style. However, he is much influenced by his close friends, some of whom are the leading trend-setters in the London clubs. So, although he is now very much divorced from his previous nightlifestyle where he was already a notorious figure known for his outrageous garb, he is certainly not out of touch.

In February this year, he described his style and taste in clothes and jewellery thus: "I don't like expensive jewellery, I'd be so worried about losing it. I really love my Monty Don necklace because it's junky but classy junk. It's Egyptian-looking which is great because it fitted in so well with the theme of our Christmas shows.

"I have all my clothes made by Dexter Wong who has a stall in Hyper Hyper, he co-designs the outfits with me, and then he makes them up ... I had a great outfit made out of a bedspread covered in numbers which I bought in Spain.

"I'm really into platforms at the moment. I was being pestered by this sports company called Puma to wear their shoes, so one day I was in this restaurant in Germany and designed a pair of shoes on the serviette and said if they could make them, I'd wear them. I drew a sort of pair of platform running shoes and I never thought they'd do it ... but they did!"

George is very fond of motifs, from Hebrew squiggles, to numbers, to the famous dollar sign jacket which he wore on his recent tour of America and also made the front page of nearly every national daily newspaper.

He is currently working on his own collection of clothes which will be off-the-peg, cheap and easily available. "I'm going back into fashion. That's something I've always wanted to do. I'm doing the designing with a machinist who's very clever. The clothes have dollars and pounds signs on them. It's very topical in that there's a lot of poverty around at the moment ... I'm thinking all the time about how cheap we can make them. They'll be in the shops but they won't be called Boy George clothes."

The machinist he mentions is Liz Flynn who is second in command at

Wendy Dagworthy's small, self-sufficient and successful empire. She says of the dollar sign jacket: "It was made out of some material he'd picked up somewhere for £1 and another jacket was made out of shower curtain material. I made all the lamé suits for the band . . . he's very easy to deal with, he knows exactly what he wants."

George's latest favourite item of clothing is a tartan kilt which he has been wearing over Katherine Hamnett's tracksuit-type outfits, with added slogans bearing conscientious social comments such as: SAVE THE WORLD, CHOOSE LIFE, and similar pro CND sentiments.

The tartan kilt worn over tracksuit bottoms (preferably BodyMap) is an idea which George has borrowed from his style-conscious friends. These die-hard club-goers made a fresh start to the year by disposing of their fake dreadlocks, ghettoblasters, Fila, Lacoste and Nike "casual" wear and sportswear, although the tracksuit remained but was modified. Punk priestess Poly Styrene's 1978 prophesy came true – "the world turned Day-Glo" – for a couple of months at least.

The major club fashion for the early part of 1984 was Day-Glo and Diamanté. It began with subtle (if they can be called that) accessories such as pea-green socks, gloves and small woolly hats. The wet gloomy Winter streets of London positively glowed and throbbed with colour. Fiorucci came back to the fore and to the rescue of the day-glo crazies, by being the first to open a new shop on the King's Road to supply (exclusively for a while) complete day-glo outfits, predominantly in green, but also yellow and orange. This was a screaming reaction to the black Gothic leather and studs Batcave/Punk hangers-on look which had haunted the King's Road for far too long. It was obvious that fashion was going to go from the austere extreme to the glamorous extreme. OK, so hard times were here and here to stay, but who wants to admit it? Diamanté earrings and bracelets became *de rigueur*, the bigger, longer, danglier, the better. Huge diamanté brooches were *a must* to be pinned to the front right lapel of your Katherine Hamnett jacket. Most fake paste jewellery was obtained from Butler & Wilson which has been supplying people from Lulu to Boy George, for years. But the most important accessory to bear in mind here, was the sex of the person wearing the paste. Yes, it was the season of the rhinestone rent*boy*, male jewellery certainly "came out" in its own right.

That much-maligned and misused fabric which gave punk a bad name – fake leopard-skin – made a stylish re-appearance via Annie Lennox's Catwoman/Kitka look with masculine

● *Katharine Hamnett's influence has adapted the casuals and modified the ubiquitous tracksuit giving it back the status it lost to the mass market. Photo by Mark Lebon.*

● *Inset, fur fabric reclaimed its style from the punks. Designed by Lucy Thompson. Photo by Peter Williams.*

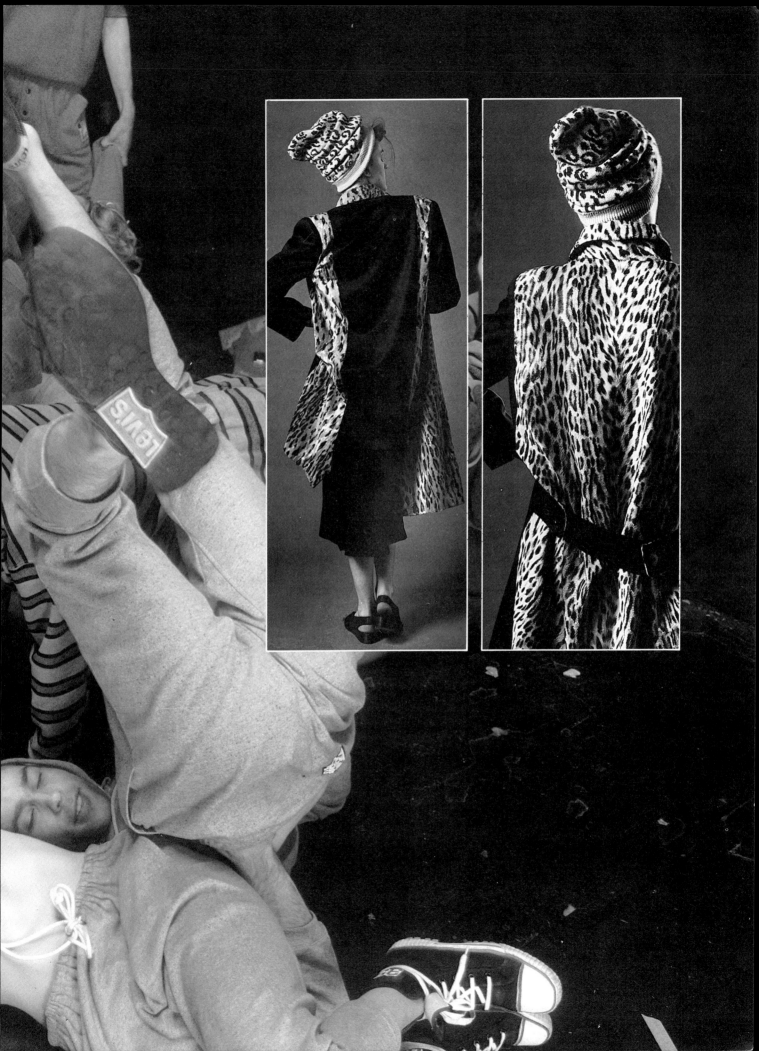

*eft, Leigh Bowery.   A synthetic synthesis of
venties prostitute style and the Indian gods.
Photo by Sheila Rock.*

*Knocked up by a Singer, underneath the paste
and glitter the most important accessory was
the sex. Photo by Jill Furmanovsky.*

jackets and Kossack style pillbox hats, all in fake fur.

As day-glo hit the high streets and thus the chain-stores, it became out-of date (or in club speak "naff") over-night. In March, the pea-green socks were replaced by glitter socks, prefer-ably in silver or blue. Beetle crushers have been dug out of attics, dusted down and customised with spray-can-paint-mini-graffiti. Bright yellow-over-red tartan suits with trousers cropped high above the ankle were run up at home on the Singer out of material chosen from Borovicks, a fabric shop in Soho which is the best stocked and most popular amongst the fashion designers, fashion students, home dressmaker and popstars. Judy Blame's rubber "nuclear fallout" jewellery mingled and mangled the diamanté necklaces and bracelets.

The very latest and most bizarre fashion at the time of writing to emerge from the London club scene has borrowed from and expanded on the glam rock theme combined with Indian influences. Two much photo-graphed and talked about leaders of this outrageous style are Leigh Bowery and Trojan. Leigh is the most outspoken of the two – he sports blue face and body make-up, enormous rubberised platform shoes, oversize shirts with four or six sleeves and leatherette caps decorated with diam-anté, sequins, pearls and stars.

A fashion designer from Melbourne, Australia, who emigrated for safety's sake to England about three years ago, he sells to talent-spotter Suzanne Bartsch in New York, and his new line will soon be available in Nostalgia of Mud. He explains where he gets his inspiration from:

"The green and blue make-up comes from the Indian Gods, the statues of gods like Vishnu and Shiva are in blue and red. They're also drip-ping in jewellery, every available place on the body to put pearls and jewels – you'll find them there. Also, because the gods have got lots of arms, I got the idea to make tops with extra sleeves and things, but Rachel Auburn has started doing that now and selling them in Browns. I particu-larly like synthetic materials, you can get very intense colours with nylon. I used a lot of tartans and fun-fur combined with the Seventies prosti-tute look such as huge platforms and fake snake-skin in my latest show (New York, April 1984). I'm exper-imenting in a totally new form of make-up, the idea is derived from Picasso's Cubist paintings, it's hard to describe really, but I draw a long black line down one side of my face and then draw an extra nose . . . it's very interesting visually, I'm not bothered about whether I look pretty or not."

Street fashion goes dada . . . where can it possibly go from here?

NEIL MATTHEWS

designer profile: ronaldus shamask

Marina Sturdza

● New York designer Ronaldus Shamask is often described as a "European" designer and he has been frequently compared to Italy's Gian Franco Ferre, probably because they share a disciplined, thoughtful and architectural approach to fashion. The comparison is intended as a compliment, but the fact is, Ronaldus Shamask is very much his own man and his designs resemble no one else's.

Shamask has a very personal vision of fashion, and he's passionately enthusiastic about his philosophy, which he recently elaborated upon in his sun-washed, white-floored Madison Avenue headquarters. "I don't do ruffles, sequins or bows," Shamask shudders. "Cut and proportion are all I care about. Everything in my clothing must have a function. I try to pare down, to remove all extraneous detail so that my designs are reduced almost to sculptural shapes." Indeed, "less is more" might well be Shamask's personal credo. His approach to fashion is comparable to a ritualistic Japanese tea ceremony, a high, cerebral exercise. Indeed, Shamask is fascinated by all things oriental; his Japanese friends are legion and he

spends much of his own spare time at Manhattan's Japan House, absorbing oriental art, films and music while learning to comprehend the oriental mind and culture. "I have learned an incredible amount from the Japanese attitude toward design. I have learned to be receptive, to acknowledge a different way of looking at things and to let things grow on me."

Ronaldus Shamask is the consummate perfectionist. Each and every garment he creates is a painstaking labour of love, its production sometimes necessitating as many as five or six fitting toiles until Shamask is completely satisfied with every line, curve, the fall of the fabric, and the cutting and seaming solution. Such an investment of time and effort would

likely make the profit-oriented or the mass-marketers shudder, but it has served Shamask extremely well. In the five short years he's been designing for his own company, Moss/Shamask, he has parlayed his elegant, spare and exquisitely structured clothes all the way up the fashion stratosphere. Fashion experts have unanimously praised his spare, intricately cut garments, and his clothes are regularly featured in the major international fashion magazines.

At first glance, Shamask's designs are lean and clean, ultra-linear in their look, almost monastic in form. But appearances are deceiving and the apparent simplicity often belies the intricacy and complexity of every individual design. Herein lies the key to Shamask's singular style. He has always eschewed traditional cutting and pattern-making techniques, adopting what might be called a "Zen" approach to clothing, reducing and paring away all non-essential details of construction, preferring to incorporate shape and movement into every garment by devising entirely original cutting and seaming techniques, analyzing the material characteristics, the resilience and resistance of each fabric and using its properties to maximum effect to achieve small miracles such as his 1982 red wool coat, which was shaped from a single piece of spiral-cut and seamed fabric, a garment which may qualify as the most photographed design, by any designer in recent memory.

Much of Shamask's success may be attributed to the fact that he is blessed with admirable personal discipline and has had the maturity to pace himself, never biting off more than he can chew at any one time, and expanding only after careful consideration. As well, his relationship with friend and partner Murray Moss is a fortuitous one, a complimentary marriage of taste and talent that is almost seamless. Says Shamask, "We overlap perfectly – I respond to Murray's opinions on design, and he listens to my ideas about business and merchandising. What's more, I know that if Murray were to make a personal selection from a thousand possible choices, they would invariably be identical to mine."

At thirty-eight, Shamask is pale and slender, with deep-set eyes that gaze with great intensity directly at you. He takes great pains to convey his exact meaning, elaborating and adding detail to every statement, like a painter adding final embellishments. His discourse is liberally punctuated with references to music, literature, painting, poetry and all things Japanese. His tastes are eclectic and esoteric, and he's intensely concerned with presentation, be it in his home,

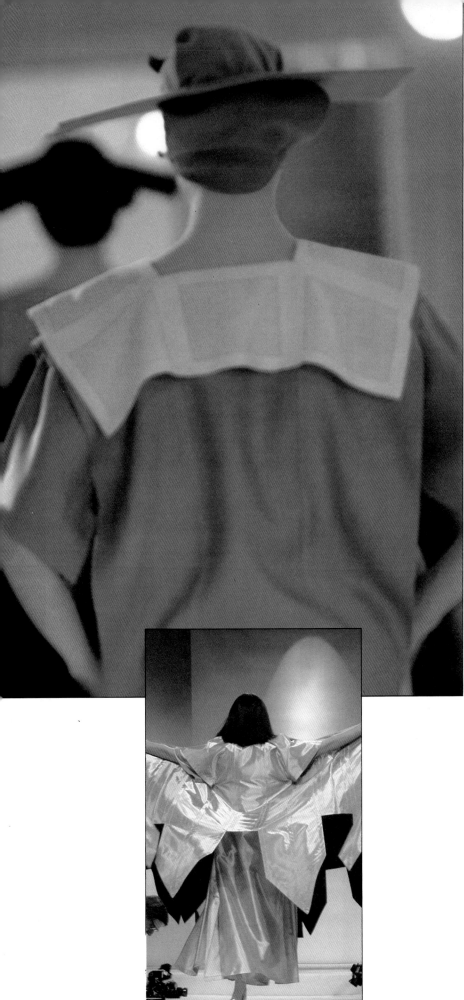

in his studio, for his showroom, store or his fashion shows. In his very first collection, he startled the audience with the languorous pace of his presentation, a speed dictated in part by the fact that he could afford only six mannequins. But it was a small moment of civility, a notable respite from the normally frenzied pace of New York fashion shows, and the models' slow, measured steps enabled the audience to really appreciate the details.

Of late, the earnest, somewhat introverted Shamask has become rather more gregarious. Success and its attendant security has liberated a warmth and humour he used rarely to reveal. Even his decidedly intellectual approach to fashion appears to have loosened up. "I am discovering texture and colour really for the first time. I used to think colour and texture were secondary and I performed intellectual somersaults to create different effects. I was so involved, and so preoccupied with structure that my designs were sometimes a little bleak." (Indeed, for several reasons, Shamask stuck to three colours only – a limited palette of white/black/red, explaining that financial strictures made it impossible to work with a larger number of fabrics and colours.)

"Now, my response is more organic and much less cerebral. However, I have discovered that you don't have to re-invent the wheel every time, that texture and colour can help convey emotion and feeling." While Shamask is visibly more relaxed and spontaneous, and claims he is having a lot more fun, he cautions that the angst of preparing four collections a year (two for his own signature line and two for the moderately priced Cuddlecoat line) only increases with success. "The danger is to get complacent, to start doing what other people expect. The moment you stop taking risks, you stop growing."

Inevitably, success and high

visibility brings in its share of plagiarists and emulators, a fact that makes the normally soft-spoken Shamask seethe. "I get very upset whenever we take a risk, introduce something totally new . . . and then I see that the entire industry is just waiting to pounce on it. If there was a law against copying, the whole industry would collapse. In fact, fashion is built on the premise of stealing designs. There may be only six designers in the entire world that take genuine risks."

Shamask's background is anything but fixated on fashion. He's already proved himself an eclectic designer and claims he sees little difference between clothing, industrial and interior design. "Successful design of any kind always starts with function and need – the art and styling come from the sensitivity you bring to that function."

Shamask comes by his originality honestly and has earned his right to fashion independence by proving his ability and enterprise in a wide variety of design disciplines, which he has successfully practiced in such improbable locations as Amsterdam, Melbourne, Buffalo and Paris.

The Dutch-born designer has had an admittedly wide-ranging career. He grew up in the Australian outback, where his family had emigrated in the Fifties. Later, he moved to Melbourne and worked in display design. Returning to England, he met an old friend who had become a successful illustrator. Shamask, needing a job, figured he could do at least as well, tried his hand at a couple of drawings (he'd absolutely no training in illustration) and was hired on the spot. Four years later, he headed back to Holland where his work soon attracted international attention, and he was asked to come to North America to join the world-famous "Company of Man" in Buffalo, to work on theatre sets and production. Although his previous theatrical experience was limited to a few

designs for the Australian ballet, his flair and talent were already evident.

Shamask stayed three years, as resident designer, responsible for sets, costumes, posters and promotional and print material, then moved to New York to pursue his painting. The early Seventies found him painting, designing interiors and designing clothing for a growing list of private clients, one of whom even insisted he design furs for her, which were then executed by the prestigious New York furrier, Maximilian. "It was such a wonderful time; I was living on whatever I could – I had such fun, and I received commissions to design everything from cutlery to clothing."

A few short years ago, Shamask happened to see an exhibit of Charles James clothes, the eccentric and brilliant U.S. designer, "I saw then that clothes could actually be a form of art, and it was an art I wanted to explore."

Never one to let the grass grow under his feet, Shamask rapidly produced twelve muslins, found a group of backers and selected a partner in business, the ex-Shakespearian actor named Murray Moss, with whom he is still happily associated. He produced two entire couture seasons, working single-handedly on his dining room table, with the assistance of a single seamstress. "I really had to start from scratch, and I had to resolve the problems on a small scale. Initially, I was too rigid in my approach; it took me years to learn spontaneity."

When Shamask was finally satisfied, he and Moss compiled a list of twenty-five speciality stores, and travelled around the country showing them their wares. Those fine stores are still the nucleus of their clientele.

Most recently, Shamask has signed a spectacular contract with Mitsukoshi, the Japanese mega-manufacturer, to produce an extensive collection to be introduced this fall. For the first time, he is going to his beloved Japan, a prospect he is deliriously

excited about. He is also designing shoes for Bruno Menatti, after regretfully relinquishing his earlier design contract with Italy's Colette shoes. "It was difficult to do it long distance and the Italian lasts weren't well-suited to the American foot."

Shamask is articulate and garrulous, generous with his opinions:

On criticism, he says: "It's never really easy to accept. I listen to everyone, I hear what they say, and I form my own opinion of what's valid and what's not."

On being called "an architectural designer": "The fashion world is suffering from insecurity – it's always looking for labels."

On people who influenced him most: "Charles James first made me realize that fashion was a valid form of design. Stella Blum at the Metropolitan Museum, who taught me so much. Editors such as Nonnie Morre, Carrie Donovan and Andre Leontelli and photo-reporter Bill Cunningham – they were the first to encourage me and to understand my efforts."

On leisure: "I am learning to take time for myself. It is important to take breaks, to remove yourself and change projects. A new design project is one of my greatest forms of relaxation."

On the customers: "I am old-fashioned. I believe public awareness and contact is important. That is why I will always keep a retail outlet of my own . . . I want to know what people are thinking and saying about my clothes, whether they can move freely, whether they like the shapes or not."

On fashion obsolescence: "I don't want my clothes to look like last year or two years ago or next year. I think it is important to design something that has a future."

As for Shamask himself, what is likely to be in his future? One sure bet is men's wear, which he plans to introduce in short order.

What would he have done if he hadn't become a fashion designer? "I want to go back to art sometime. Clothes are three-dimensional; now I want to try sculpturing instead of painting. For me, challenge and pleasure are inseparable – there are still a lot of things I would like to do."

No doubt Shamask will be doing them all, and well, in the years to come.

THE CONTRIBUTORS

● SHERIDAN McCOID
was fashion assistant on *Honey*
magazine and the London *Evening
Standard*. She is now fashion assistant
on *The Guardian*.

● JACKIE MOORE
is London fashion editor of the
Glasgow Herald, woman's page editor
of the *Countryside* group of
magazines, fashion editor of the
Dorchester Magazine and a contributor
to *The Birmingham Post*, the *Yorkshire
Post* and *Ambassador Magazine*.

● BRENDA POLAN
worked on *Woman's Own* magazine
as sub-editor and then moved to
Woman as assistant features editor.
Since 1977 she has been with *The
Guardian* where she is now fashion
editor.

● LORNA KOSKI
was born in Hawaii. She was
educated at Harvard and Cambridge
universities and is currently fashion
features editor at *Women's Wear
Daily*.

● HARRIS GAFFIN
is a freelance photographer who
works and lives in Tokyo and New
York. He knows the Japanese fashion
scene intimately and contributes
regularly to *Women's Wear Daily*. He
has given talks and slide
presentations on Japanese Fashion.
Prior to this he worked in
Scandinavia as a freelance lecturer
giving slide shows on American
lifestyles.

● IAIN R WEBB
studied fashion at St Martin's School
of Art. Since graduating in 1980 he
has been employed as a "finger on
the pulse hipster" by such
magazines as *Company*, *Cosmopolitan*,
i-D, *Time Out*, *Over 21*, *You
Magazine* and *NME*. He is at present
style editor of *Blitz*.

● KAREN MOLINE
is fashion writer for New York's
Village Voice and freelance for music
magazines across America. She is

currently writing *A History of Hats*
and a series of adventure novels
starring Lois Lane. Her favorite
pastime is hanging out on Manhattan
street corners.

● NATHALIE CAVENDISH
has been working as a stylist, mainly
in advertising stills for the last eight
years. ● NATHALIE LAMORAL,
her alter ego, has contributed to *The
Observer*, *The New York Times
Magazine*, *Elle*, *Harpers & Queen* and
Decoration International as a fashion
reportage photographer.

● LYDIA KEMENY
studied at St Martin's and the Royal
College of Art. She started
professional life at *Vogue* and
subsequently worked for numerous
publications, advertising agencies
and design companies. She began
teaching full-time at St Martin's in
1972 and became Head of Fashion/
Textiles at St Martin's in 1976.

● PERCY SAVAGE
won a scholarship to take his Master
of Arts degree at the Ecole des
Beaux Arts in Paris. He then worked
as a journalist and illustrator for the
Journal de Geneve and the continental
edition of *The Daily Mail*, while also
being a textile designer for Staron
and Bianchini Ferrier. His career in
PR began at Lanvin Castillo, then
Nina Ricci and the Chambre
Syndicale de la Haute Couture. Yves
St Laurent brought him to London
for the launch of the Rive Gauche
shops. He is currently a specialist
PR for men's and women's fashions,
perfumes and cosmetics, furs and
furriers and contributes to a number
of international publications.

● CARY LABOVITCH
● SIMON TESLER
are the publishers and editors of
Blitz, one of the new generation of
youth culture lifestyle magazines.
Founded in September 1980 by
Carey Labovitch, a second-year
student at Oxford University, and
winner of the Guardian/NUS Best
Graphics Award in 1981, *Blitz*
became professional in the Autumn
of 1982. The present editorial staff
of three are all under 25 years of age.

● TED POLHEMUS
is an anthropologist specialising in
non-verbal communication, clothing
and adornment. He is the editor of
Social Aspects of the Human Body and
co-editor of *The Body as a Medium of
Expression*. A frequent commentator
on radio and television, he also writes
and takes photographs for a wide
range of newspapers and magazines

● LYNN PROCTER is an actress,
journalist and photographer.
Together with Ted Polhemus, she
has written *Fashion and Anti-Fashion*
and *Popstyles*.

● CYNTHIA ROSE
is a freelance contributing editor to
New Musical Express and writes for
several music papers including
American *Creem* magazine.

● TONY STEWART is deputy
editor of *New Musical Express* and
was editor of *The Jam: A Beat
Concerto*. They worked together on
*Cool Cats: 25 Years of Rock 'N' Roll
Style*.

● CONNY JUDE
Freelance illustrator for six years . . .
never out of work yet (touch wood).
Jobs from *Time Out*, Malcolm
McLaren cover to Evian billboards
. . . Now working for European
exhibition in Versailles. Likes: Red
. . . Leather . . . Black . . . Leather
. . . Dogs. Dislikes: smell of pipe
tobacco . . . tinned fruit and veg . . .
child molesters.

● FIONA RUSSELL POWELL
was expelled from public school at
the age of 15. She moved from her
home town of Sheffield to London
where she lived in the famous
Carburton Street squat. Now 21, she
writes for several music publications
and is a major contributor to *The
Face*.

● MARINA STURDZA
is a fashion columnist and
contributor to the Toronto Star,
the Ottawa Citizen, the Edmonton
Journal, the Vancouver Sun,
Harpers Bazaar France, the Los
Angeles Herald Examiner and
the Miami Herald.